Activate Your Life
50 Transformational Exercises From Coaches Around the World

First Printing 2018

ISBN: 9781728826295

Published by
The Art of Adventure
146 Helfenstein Ave
St. Louis, MO 63119
Derekloudermilk.com

Edited by Word and Wing
wordandwing.co

WORD & WING

Disclaimer:

This book is not intended as a substitute for the medical advice of physicians. The reader should regularly consult a physician in matters relating to his/her health and particularly with respect to any symptoms that may require diagnosis or medical attention. The information provided in Activate You Life is for educational and informational purposes only, and is made available to you as self-help tools for your own use. The Authors cannot and do not guarantee that you will attain a particular result, and you accept and understand that results differ by each individual.

TABLE OF CONTENTS

Acknowledgements

If you get the right people together, amazing things happen. I want to thank the awesome team behind this project:

Tyler Wagner – Mentor, Founder of Authors Unite
Diane Hopkins - Editor
Cassandra Galbier – Project Manager
Leo Castrence – Sales and Marketing
Rachel Leahy – Project Manager
Ona Regnier – Project Manager
Hamid Alwassi - Marketing

Want to Write A Chapter In The Next Activate Your Life Book?

visit us at
www.activateyourlifebook.com/2nd-edition/
and fill out a registration form.

Introduction

How Activate Your Life came to be

Activate Your Life was initiated as a project to share the work of amazing coaches, to help them become published authors, and to give you access to a collection of the best coaching exercises.

Three years ago, I was part of a collaborative book project where 100 entrepreneurs shared a key business lesson in their own chapter in *The Better Business Book, Volume I*. The book became a bestseller and gave me the confidence to publish my first solo book, Superconductors.

As a coach, many of my peers are incredibly talented coaches and have created their own methodologies that help people achieve breakthroughs in many areas of their lives. In addition to hosting the *Art of Adventure Podcast*, I see this book as another way I can help shine the light on the work of these coaches.

When I first started as an entrepreneur, a few simple exercises changed my life. One such exercise was to envision my perfect day in detail. Three years later, I was watching the sunset over the Adriatic with my family, and I realized that I had just lived out my exact perfect day. Going through an exercise can truly activate your life.

How to use this book

We have broken down the content into different sections with certain themes – I recommend going straight to the section that most interests you or where you think you can find the biggest benefit.

These exercises are all about action. You "work through" them. You will get the biggest benefit by setting aside some time and completing an exercise. If you don't set aside time to do them, you won't get the benefit.

It can help to know that when you are working on a transformational process, it will likely feel uncomfortable. This is because your brain is working hard to create new connections as you learn, your worldview may be shifting, and you may have to use courage if you face challenging truths. Anytime our physical body or thoughts are changed, it interrupts the careful balance called homeostasis, which takes energy. Learn to embrace this discomfort or struggle, because this means the exercises are working!

To keep your momentum, it can help to have a strong emotional attachment with the outcome you are seeking. Check back in with WHY you are doing these exercises in the first place? What is the vision you see for yourself? Who needs you to show up and do your best with these exercises?

If you are a coach, welcome! After starting this project, we soon discovered that we were all really excited to find out and start using everyone else's exercises. Please feel free to try out, use, and adapt these exercises with your own clients. You could even build out the curriculum for your events using these exercises. If you would like to republish any particular exercise, please contact the individual author.

This book gives you access to a team of the world's top coaches, in the comfort of your own home. This is a great book to bring to your mastermind or networking group or do with an accountability buddy. As with the African proverb, "To go fast, go alone. To go far, go with friends". You can go far with this book, but if you are truly motivated to transform your life, I encourage you to seek continued support from coaches. All of our authors offer additional training and programs, so if you want more from a particular coach, please visit their website or email them directly.

We hope Activate Your Life will help you breakthrough your most pressing challenges and guide you to achieve your biggest goals.

Derek Loudermilk,

Art of Adventure

PART 1: MIND AND EMOTIONS

Mindset - Inner dialogue – Emotional freedom

THE DIALOGUE MODALITY: CHANGE YOUR MIND & YOUR EMOTIONS BY SPEAKING DIRECTLY TO THEM

By Brendan Burns

The Dialogue Modality allows you to speak directly to an emotion, thought, person, limiting belief, or anything else causing you pain in your life. Using this powerful tool, you can process and release any limitation holding you back so you can move forward and create the life you deserve. It's for anyone looking for a process that can be used on a daily basis to make a change or life improvement.

Great for:

- People who tend to identify with their negative emotions or thought patterns
- People ready to break free from limiting beliefs or lack of motivation
- People who are holding themselves back because of things they believe to be true about themselves

– – –

The Dialogue Modality is an opportunity to speak directly with an emotion, thought, person, limiting belief or anything causing you pain in your life to get to the root of the issue.

Many of us subconsciously and consistently identify with negative emotions or destructive thought patterns, and as a result those thoughts and feelings can anchor themselves inside of our brains and nervous system, creating a destructive pattern that can impact us for years.

Much in the same way that a person who is severely out of shape might think, "Oh no, I'm not a runner" or "I could never do that," when you identify with negative emotions or consistent debilitating thoughts, you begin to believe them to be true. You then buy into your ego-based unconsciousness and let it taint your truth. You may propagate this by saying (and believing) things like "I am an angry person" or "I'm always anxious" and this cements it inside your head.

To redefine your negative thoughts and break this pattern, you need to distinguish yourself from the emotion or thought process causing the pain. This can be accomplished using the Dialogue Modality, which is a written or spoken exercise that consists of having a conversation with the painful trigger or feeling itself.

The dialogue should be held between you and the emotion that you are experiencing. First, name the emotion, thought or habit that you are working with. For example, you might be dealing with a lot of anger and therefore you name your sub-personality Angry Guy (AG) or Anger (A). Naming this part of you, which isn't really you, helps stop your identification with it and begins to allow you to see it as a separate entity that can be processed and released from your body and mind. Once you begin to name and speak with your sub-personalities, you can control them, get rid of them, and transform them into positive thoughts and actions.

Once the problem has been identified and named, you then begin to write a back-and-forth discussion with that emotion or thought pattern as a way to convert the negative energy of that persona that you have created into a more positive emotion or something better.

Below is an example between a client Daniel and his Angry Guy Sub-personality. Daniel has been suffering from frequent debilitating anger and is ready to do a dialogue so he can process and release it:

Daniel: You have been so angry lately and it is affecting me very negatively.

Angry Guy: That's my job. We have to be angry, especially when things don't go our way.

6

Daniel: I hear and feel your anger and it is causing problems in my relationship and in my interactions with others.

Angry Guy: Good, screw them! We need to be angry.

Daniel: No, we can stop. We can release that anger in healthier ways. I can journal and take deep breaths. And I can remind myself that everything is okay.

Angry Guy: No way, we have to get angry and get back at these people screwing us over.

Daniel: We can settle this by watching how we think. We can remind ourselves that the actions of others cause us to think upsetting thoughts that aren't true. We can self-soothe in these moments.

Angry Guy: I don't know, I'm not sure about this.

Daniel: Just try. Try to soothe ourselves and release the anger. Okay?

Angry Guy: Okay

Use these 5 steps for yourself:

1. **Identify the "sub-personality"**
   Begin by identifying the "sub-personality," which can be a negative emotion, person, or thought that you are experiencing. For example, if you are very afraid about your finances, the sub-personality could be Fear of Money (FoM) or Finances Guy (FG).

2. **Prepare the Dialogue**
   Now get a pen and paper, Word document, or whatever you are most comfortable with. Write on the piece of paper "Me:" on one line and "Sub-personality:" on the next line.

3. **Have the sub-personality start the conversation**
   Start the conversation, beginning with the negative sub-personality that needs to be confronted. For example, the conversation might start: "Guilty Guy: Why aren't you going to George's wedding? You should feel so guilty and awful."

4. **Respond positively from you to the sub-personality**
   Next, write out a direct response to the sub-personality, coming from a place of love, kindness, peace and truth.

   An example response might be: "Me: We've grown apart over the years and no longer share similar values. I am choosing to put myself first and protect myself from people who are bad influences."

5. **Continue the Dialogue until it feels complete**
   Continue a back-and-forth discussion with your sub-personality until you have worked through the issue and transformed the negative thought into a positive one.

Tips for doing a Dialogue

Dialogues are especially useful if you are self-identifying with compulsions or negative emotions. It gives you a way to disassociate yourself from the issue and find positive solutions to transform your negative thoughts and behaviors.

Try to stay focused and not to give up on the exercise until complete. Note: This exercise should not take pages and pages to write. You should be able to complete a dialogue in only 8-10 lines. The challenge is to face your negative thoughts and transform them into positive ones.

Doing the dialogue is just the first step. Here are some follow-up tips:

- Many negative sub-personalities will require revisiting. One dialogue is usually insufficient to release it.

- Save all of your dialogues for later review. Set aside a time once a week to review your recent dialogues. Journal and write a reflection after reading them.

- Share a dialogue with a spouse or loved one, if appropriate, for support.

DYNAMIC SPIN RELEASE™ FOR INSTANT EMOTIONAL SHIFTS

By Helene Weiss

Dynamic Spin Release soothes and transforms unwanted emotions in less than 5 minutes. It helps you get out of an unresourceful emotional state and opens your mind to see and consider new options. This exercise is for anyone that gets sidetracked by their emotions and wants a simple method for gaining insight and freedom.

Great for:

- People stuck in unhelpful emotions or thought patterns
- Guiding clients out of an unresourceful mental and emotional state very quickly
- Gaining insight into the subconscious representation of challenging issues

– – –

Do you often get stuck in a funk and don't find yourself able to get out of it? Maybe you're feeling agitated for no obvious reason and lash out at your partner, feeling sorry afterwards. But somehow you just can't help yourself when it happens. It's almost like an alter ego taking over.

This exercise works instantly and requires no psychological knowledge, preparation or equipment. All it requires is for you to close your eyes and tune in to what's bubbling underneath the surface. Anger? Anxiety? Fear? No worries. Since it's already there, let's say hello and play with it.

All you need to do is a fairly simple and easy to remember visualization exercise and those emotional knots will dissolve within an instant by themselves. You'll see. Simply follow the steps outlined below and allow whatever is showing up for you:

1. Close your eyes and feel into the challenging situation you're currently facing or the uncomfortable feeling you're experiencing. Find out where it's located in your body.
2. Physically grab the feeling with your hands and pull it out of your body, putting it in front of you so you can see it.
3. What does it look like: size, colour, texture, distance from the body? Is it very close by or still partly in the body? Bring it about 1 metre in front of you and out of your body.
4. Notice in which direction it is turning: clockwise or counter-clockwise? If it isn't turning, which direction would it turn if it could?
5. Halt it there and begin turning it in the other direction until it turns smoothly.
6. Then spin it faster and faster and faster and faster... until it's teared into pieces and disperses into the universe.
7. Now in the empty space that's left in front of you, a gift appears. It's a gift especially made for you at this moment in time. It can be a symbol, a person, a colour, a sound, anything.
8. Take the gift and integrate it back into the body where the uncomfortable feeling used to be.
9. Now enjoy this moment of integration and notice how it feels different.
10. Open your eyes and take a deep breath, breathing out any remaining uncomfortable feelings or sensations. Repeat the exercise if needed.

Tips for further investigation and healing:

So you've just had a great experience. Something within you has shifted. Make use of this new state of mind and emotion for further inquiry about the situation that has created this

11

feeling in the first place. What new conclusions do you draw now, about yourself and with regard to the situation?

For example, I once had a client who described that she was losing her temper very easily at work when dealing with difficult people on the phone. She felt terrible about it, but couldn't help it. It was like an outside force was taking over her and she couldn't stop herself from bursting out in anger on the phone.

To make matters worse, her boss had picked up on it and told her off. This left her paralyzed when answering the phone, because on the one hand she could feel her anger bubbling up uncontrollably when the other person responded unfavorably, on the other hand she was worried that if she'd burst out again, she would eventually lose her job.

Now the underlying issue my client was facing, the root cause of her problem, lay much deeper than what she experienced as outbursts of anger, and this is what NLP Coaching is there to detect and unwire. However, to get this client out of her initial paralyzed state of mind, which was completely closed to other options of thinking and feeling, I applied the Dynamic Spin Release™ technique.

It instantly relaxed her emotional tension, and her breathing and body posture changed into a more relaxed state. Because of the nature of the exercise where uncomfortable thoughts and feelings are transformed into what feels like a gift, the client will naturally come from a more resourceful state of mind when talking about their situation afterwards. It creates an opening ground for the practitioner to build on with further investigation and treatment.

My client suddenly saw the whole situation in a different light. She saw it as an opportunity to improve her skill set. She remembered how she liked her communication courses at university when she was younger. So she took this as an opportunity to get back into it and improve on what she had enjoyed earlier in life. She now saw those phone calls as practice units rather than "real life" situations. She also came up with strategies to help her feel more relaxed at work so that the likelihood of bursting out in anger would decrease.

Tips for coaches
This exercise is meant for clients who face challenges in their lives, and are otherwise mentally healthy. It's not meant for clients with mental disorders and depression. In some cases, you may find that a client finds it difficult to integrate the gift back into their body. This usually means that they're not quite ready yet to fully embrace all the parts of themselves and that more healing work is required.

If this happens, simply let the client lead to what feels comfortable. Some like to just look at the gift and get to know it more before doing anything else with it. Others like to touch it or hold it in their hands, or pull it to their chest and hug it. In any case, ask them what insights they're gaining from the experience about themselves and their situation, and take the session from there.

ABRACADABRA: THE MAGICAL LIFE ENHANCING POTENTIAL OF CONSTRUCTIVE DIALOGUE

By Zachary Heidemann

This exercise helps you identify destructive thought and speech patterns and feelings and replace them with constructive ones. You'll be shown a process of positive mental conditioning. It's for people who struggle with negative thinking and are ready to stop sabotaging and start supporting and nurturing their own happiness and success.

Great for:

- People who are working with the law of attraction.
- People who struggle with any of the following: low self-esteem, poor self-image, anger, depression, anxiety, chronic physical illness and/or chronic mental illness.
- People who self-sabotage or are constantly failing to succeed.

This exercise helps us realize our full creative potential and provides a reliable and effective pathway to enhance our quality of life considerably. When practiced daily, this exercise can help us to identify and heal subconscious, undesired, toxic, self-sabotaging and other unhealthy patterns and replace these with healthier patterns which enhance and optimize our lives.

Thoughts and consciousness are energy and, just like all energy, different kinds of thoughts have different frequencies with different effects on our bodies. We can literally alter the physiology of our being by choosing kind and loving thoughts in place of harsh and fearful thoughts.

When we replace the careless thoughts and speech with more deliberate thoughts and speech, the net results include:

enhanced quality of life for ourselves and those around us, feeling better about ourselves, improved relationship to self, and improved relationship to others. For example, kindness is a pattern of speaking and relating which is very cathartic, healing and encourages everyone towards resonating at that frequency.

Steps to Positive Mental Conditioning

Step 1 – While this exercise can be performed anywhere, at first it is best to practice in an environment that is conducive to meditation, self-awareness and healing. Set aside some time during meditation or yoga for this exercise.

Step 2 – Now in your preferred meditative setting, begin paying attention to the thoughts running through the mind. Be mindful and pay attention to the voice speaking and what it is saying. Pay particular attention to thoughts in which you visualize yourself speaking, either to yourself or to others, and pay careful attention to the words you are choosing. Identify how these words make you feel.

Step 3 – Compare these feelings to how you would like to feel. As soon as you identify any manner of thought or speech that does not result in the feelings you desire, you have identified the opportunity for change.

Step 4 – Make the change. Whatever was just thought or said, pause and make a "correction" by focusing on what you really want to feel, and choosing different words to evoke the desired feelings. For example, if you just made a mistake on something you are working on, and you catch yourself angrily yelling "You idiot! How could you make that mistake?" In your minds or out loud, this is your opportunity to relax into that with kindness, have a little chuckle at your anger and replace "You idiot!" with "That mistake is okay, but we can totally do better". Essentially, if a word or the way you are speaking makes you feel better, continue this way. If it makes you feel worse, change it.

Step 5 – Repeat, repeat, repeat. Daily practice and repetition are the keys to success with this exercise. As you become more disciplined, you may begin implementing this same method in your day-to-day speech. You will be surprised how well others react to you catching and correcting your speech with them during daily conversation.

It's also important to choose television/radio and friends/family that build you up with positive thoughts, while creating healthy boundaries and limiting your exposure to influences that use their speech in negative and destructive ways.

Case studies

I have some clients with chronic health and self-image issues that have struggled to find relief, and they have shared with me how this practice has changed their lives for the better.

It seems to work well for clients who struggle with chronic adrenal fatigue, lyme disease, mercury toxicity, depression, anger, poor self-esteem, unhealthy self-body image, and many other issues. We encourage them to recognize all of the places they are taking ownership of the illness or having defeating thoughts. Then they can replace their inner unhelpful dialogue with more healthier dialogue, which can speed up their recovery process:

"I have adrenal fatigue/lyme disease and I am always tired" shifts to "I am recovering from and healing adrenal fatigue/ lyme disease and finding ways to build my energy naturally. I believe fully in my body's ability to heal and I support it with healthy lifestyle and diet."

For other clients that struggle with strong emotions, "I am always sad and angry because of..." shifts to "I understand that I am feeling sadness and anger, but I am looking deeper to see what I can change to lead to my happiness and satisfaction. I believe I deserve to be and will be happy and peaceful". These clients are no longer uncontrollably subject

16

to their unexplainable emotions. They are actually able to feel and express emotions at a deeper level and honestly react and communicate with themselves and others in healthy ways.

Clients with self-esteem issues shift from "I am fat/skinny/ugly/ imperfect" to "I am beautiful because bodies come in all shapes and sizes, and I am grateful to live in, honor and care for mine (my own body)". These clients now realize how beautiful they truly are and see and feel the world in a more beautiful way.

Tips for coaches:

- This exercise is most effective with clients who are open and willing to try anything to improve or enhance the quality of their lives.
- This exercise can be first read from a book or delivered in writing, however, it is most effective when first delivered face-to-face in either a personal one-on-one setting, or an intimate group setting with specific examples relevant to the client.
- Check up with clients about this exercise regularly – monthly, bi-weekly, or weekly. Ask them to bring up specific examples they struggle with and offer better words/patterns until they are giving you examples of how they recognized and what they shifted to without having to ask them.

STOP GOING DOWN THE RABBIT HOLE OF NEGATIVE THOUGHTS

By Keegan White

This exercise helps you retrain your brain to stop going down the rabbit hole of negative thoughts, self-doubt, worry and fear. It's for anyone who finds themselves in the grips of their thoughts and can't find a way out.

Great for:

- People who spend a lot of time and energy worrying.
- People who get stuck in fear, complaining or self-doubt.
- People who want to overcome their negative thought patterns.

— — —

Going down the rabbit hole of your negative thoughts can be an energy draining and unproductive way of spending your time. Yet whether you are an entrepreneur, a stay-at-home parent, or a 9-5er you can probably identify with losing precious time and energy thinking about all of the things that could possibly go wrong or getting stuck in fear, worry, criticism, blame, anxiety or self-doubt.

These thoughts not only rob you of being able to enjoy the present moment; they prevent you from taking chances, getting into relationships, going on the vacation of your dreams, writing a book or going after that desired promotion. This exercise will help you retrain your mind from spinning into a spiral of negative thoughts and get you back into the present moment.

In order to rewire your brain, new neural pathways must be created by taking new actions and it is only through repetition and practice that those pathways can become your new way of thinking. This is a simple but extremely effective tool in retraining the mind so that you can focus your energy and time into more productive and peaceful activities.

Step 1: Cultivating Awareness
The first step in cultivating awareness of your thoughts is to pay attention to them. Most of us are walking around on autopilot not realizing the inner dialogue that is occurring between our ears. We don't realize how much that inner dialogue is actually creating our perception and our experiences.

Here are a few suggestions to start the process of becoming aware of your thoughts:

- Grab your journal: Journaling can be a wonderful tool to not only bring awareness to your thoughts, it also helps you notice the patterns of thinking that may be causing you discomfort. The process of journaling can help you to get to know yourself, your feelings and experiences better.
- Set aside quiet time: We are bombarded more than ever with external stimulation. Between cell phones beeping with emails, phone calls, text messages, and social media updates to podcasts, news shows or music in the car to internet, cable TV or streaming networks at home, we are so inundated with stimuli that most people rarely get a moment of quiet to themselves. With all of this external stimulation no wonder people are so disconnected to what is truly going on with them. Set aside quiet time to sit in silence daily. It is more beneficial to sit in silence for 5 minutes everyday than to try to meditate for 30 minutes once a week.
- Take a walk in nature: One of the quickest ways to tune into yourself to cultivate awareness is to take a walk in nature. Not only will you be able to connect with your Higher Self but you will improve your self-esteem, mood and sleep quality and decrease your stress, anxiety and fatigue.

Once you have cultivated awareness of your thoughts, ask yourself what types of thoughts are creating your anxiety, worry, self-doubt or negativity. It's important to address the underlying root cause that is creating this way of thinking so you can work through what that cause is.

For example, if you are thinking negative thoughts, understand what is underneath those thoughts by asking yourself these questions: Am I unhappy in my life? Have I had a recent life change? Am I angry at someone or something? Have I been victimized?

Understanding what lies underneath the thoughts is critical to helping you acknowledge the impact that the event or situation may be having on your life.

Step 2: Use A Mantra
Give yourself a mantra (a word or phrase) to use every time you find yourself going into a negative line of inner dialogue. I personally teach clients to use, "I'm not going to participate in this". Come up with your own mantra that is appropriate and impactful for you. The key is to create a word or phrase that you will use consistently to train your mind so you don't participate in that way of thinking anymore.

Every single time you notice yourself going down the rabbit hole of your negative thoughts, use the mantra to communicate to your mind to stop. Sometimes you may need to repeat the mantra over and over in order for your mind to get the message. This is because the brain will take the path of least resistance; meaning, the neural pathways in the brain will take the strongest and most used path to conserve mental energy. This is why you find yourself continually thinking in the same thought-pattern loop.

Step 3: Reframe your thoughts
Now that you have the awareness of the negative thought and are stopping it in its tracks by saying the mantra either out loud or in your head, you can move onto redirecting your thoughts using a reframe. A reframe is taking the negative thought and shifting it to a positive thought.

For example:

"I am not good enough" – the reframe can be "I have many talents that are x, y, z and I wonder what will happen by acknowledging this about me".

"I am so worried about my finances" – the reframe can be "I wonder what income is available to me by being open-minded" or "I create my own financial destiny".

"He never does the dishes!" – the reframe can be "What can I acknowledge about my partner that is helpful?" or "I wonder how much love and abundance I will receive when I stop criticizing my partner".

If you want to change the way you think, what you believe or how you feel, it starts with shifting your thoughts and changing how you perceive your reality. You can't control everything that happens to you but you can *control how you respond* to the situation and that includes how much time and energy you think about it and what those thoughts are.

CHANGE YOUR PERSPECTIVE, CHANGE YOUR LIFE

By Chase Boehringer

This exercise helps you shift your perspective and powerfully choose how you relate to everything and everyone in your life. It's useful for everyone but especially for people struggling to get over a disappointment, crisis or difficult life event.

Great for:

- People having trouble getting over a breakup, divorce or emotional upset.
- People struggling with depression and negative thoughts.
- People who want to move forward and feel empowered in their lives.

- - -

Your perspective is your reality. The way you view the world and the people in it (including yourself) makes up the reality you live in. Perspective can shift something that was once "bad" to "good", or a painful and disruptive memory, to a feeling of compassion and forgiveness.

Before you start thinking this is all fluff and "woo woo", I want you to give it a try yourself. Below you'll find everything you need to shift your opinion on something that is currently no longer serving you.

For example, I once had a belief that my ex-wife was satan, the lord of darkness. I had a story about what happened that made me right, and her wrong. That story made me feel like the hurt little boy who was absolutely right about everything.

I kept that story for years until I realized, fact by fact, that my own story was not only false, but it was keeping me from forgiving her.

I decided to focus on a higher truth – what *really* happened instead of what I wanted to tell myself to feel better.

I invite you to see your own difficult situation in a new light. Make a choice to seek out the truth in the story even if it feels more comfortable to be the victim. It's worth it.

So take a challenging situation or a person in your life – one that you think could be resolved or at least improved by having a new perspective.

It could be that you think your boss is undermining you at work, it could be the idea that your parents didn't raise you the way you think you should have been raised or, it could be your perspective on life itself.

Do you believe the world is working for you, even in the toughest times? Or do you believe life is hard, and people only care about themselves?

The perspective we have on our life, the world, and our place in it, can drastically alter the direction of our lives, and the level of happiness and fulfillment we experience during our short time on Earth.

I was once an overweight, divorced, depressed and suicidal caregiver. I believed that my ex-wife was the cause of all my problems, and life was not only hard, but not worth living anymore. That perspective almost took my life until I realized that everything had been stripped away, and although it hurt, it also meant that my life was a blank canvas, and I could create something new, anything I wanted. I could be and do anything because every day that I spend now is the "extra innings" of life.

My perspective went from hopeless and hard, to limitless. As you'd suspect, when my internal perspective shifted, my entire life shifted. From never leaving the country, to traveling the world living my dream life, finding myself and forgiveness along the way.

Below you will read the steps you can take to shift your perspective on just about anything. First you need to know one thing. There is a big difference between what is absolutely true about a situation or a person, and what is an opinion.

For example you could say: "I'm lazy. I wake up at noon and never get my work done. There's no way I can start my own business, I can hardly work a job!"

The absolute truth in that would be: "I wake up at noon."

The opinions are: "I'm lazy, I never get my work done (never is likely an opinion, let's be honest), there's no way I can start my own business, I can hardly work a job!"

As you can see, most of what we think is simply an opinion. It's our ego mind taking over, which is almost never a good thing.

A potential shift in perspective would be finding something in-between what actually happened and the opinions you've made about it. Something like "Recently I've been waking up later than I'd like, and slacking off at work. It's something I'm excited to change because I know that if I can show up the way I want in my career, it will give me the confidence I need to do it in my own business as well."

Consciously shifting our perspectives to work for us, not against us.

In order to consciously shift your perspective, you must first become aware of your perspective and take a hard look at what you've made up, and what is real. Once you've taken a hard look, the real architecting of your world and your place in it can begin.

Steps

1. Decide on a subject you feel you'd like to shift your perspective on. It could be a situation, another person, or yourself.

2. Write down your current beliefs. One or two sentences is enough.
3. Write down everything that actually happened or is absolutely true on one piece of paper, or section of a whiteboard.
4. On a separate piece of paper or section, write down everything that is an opinion. Make sure you really analyze what is an absolute fact and what is an opinion. Just because you think they or you are something, doesn't mean it's a fact.
5. On a new blank sheet start writing your new truth, the one that supports you moving forward. This represents the shift you consciously want to make.
6. Look at the process again and see where you were being a victim of circumstance and holding onto old ways of being. Choose to begin thinking in terms of your new story, knowing that your old story simply wasn't serving you anymore.

Tips

Using a whiteboard can be very helpful because you're able to look at all of it out in front of you. The process can be challenging by yourself at first because sometimes you may not be able to fully tell the difference between fact and opinion. We've been living with these truths for so long we believe they are fact, when in reality, it's half fact, half opinion. Now you get to shift what needs to be shifted in order to move forward in any area of your life.

FACING FEAR AND PERFECTIONISM WITH SELF-COMPASSION

By Jennifer Rhodes

This exercise gives you action-oriented advice to deal with issues stemming from fear and perfectionism using the latest research on self-compassion to set you up for success. It's for anyone that struggles with perfectionism, anxiety or worry or is working too hard to force success.

Great for:

- People who are perfectionists or highly anxious
- People with huge fears around money
- People undergoing a major life transition
- People resisting necessary change

– – –

"Develop success from failures. Discouragement and failure are two of the surest stepping stones to success." – Dale Carnegie

Perfectionism is common in our Western culture but few of us are aware of how much damage perfectionism can do to our psychological well-being and chances of success. When we are constantly striving for what we believe is "perfect" and "right", we miss the opportunity to develop the resilience necessary to actually be successful.

In her work, Dr. Kristen Neff highlights this resilience gap, stating that the focus of perfectionistic thinking often stems from the inevitable comparison trap we fall into while we are trying to build our self-esteem or *perceived* value. Our self-esteem is often *contingent* on career success or failure, and the race toward acquiring self-esteem can lead to fear and perfectionistic thinking that we are simply not good enough to be successful.

Learning how to be self-compassionate trains you to be able to self-soothe, like a great parent does for an upset child. Dr Neff's research has shown that increased self-compassion skills increases emotional resilience, decreases narcissism and anger and leads to more accurate self-appraisal of strengths and weaknesses. It is also the antidote to perfectionistic thinking.

This exercise will train you to become more self-compassionate so you can approach life with less fear and perfectionism.

Step 1: Get yourself grounded
Many perfectionistic individuals are anxious and spin their wheels to keep up with the stress of life. They are smart and successful but often have been told that they get in their own way when change or a challenge presents itself. Your environment matters. Putting yourself in a quiet location (preferably near nature) without other distractions will help you feel safe enough to explore what your anxiety is really about.

Step 2: Spend 15 minutes meditating
Spend 15 minutes sitting quietly meditating about the issue you are struggling with and simply notice what comes up for you. If you need to focus on something, focus on your breathing. Notice how many counts it takes you to breathe in and how many counts to breathe out. If your mind is really spinning, try to lengthen the exhale.

Step 3: Ask yourself how stressful the issue is
On a scale of 1 to 10, rate your stress on this issue. Getting a ranking of how bad the issue is for you will help guide you out of the emotional nature of fear and into a place where you are able to work with your thoughts.

Step 4: Start writing using the prompt, "What do you think you are afraid of?"
Wait for a response and simply start writing. Do not edit. Just sit with a pen and a piece of paper and start writing whatever comes up.

Step 5: Imagine yourself 10 years into the future
Next, read the following question, "I would like you to imagine for a moment that it is 10 years from now and you are past this challenge and you are having a cup of coffee with a loving friend. What would you and this friend want to say to yourself about this difficult time?" Sit and start writing your response.

Step 6: Write a compassionate letter to yourself
Next, write a compassionate letter to yourself from the standpoint of being 10 years past the issue. I have found letter writing to be a powerful way to process fear and other emotions that may have you stuck. Can you now help yourself see the strengths and weaknesses in the situation?

Step 7: Re-rate your stress level
Rate your stress level again on a scale of 1 to 10 to check your progress.

Step 8: Go out and do something fun before returning back to work
Joy is a necessary part of creative problem solving. Staying with negative feelings too long does not help solve your problems but only continues to fuel your fear and anxiety. Taking mindful breaks for joy will help you learn to regulate your emotions better over time and will decrease the need to use perfectionism as a way to cope with your anxiety.

Case study
A 35-year-old female client is struggling financially and feeling stuck with her business. She feels like a failure and worries that she is far behind her peers. She wonders whether it is time to give up her entrepreneurial dreams and get a full-time job. In a previous session, exercises to help her problem-solve only increased her frustration. For this coaching session, you have decided to meet with her in a quiet park in the hope that nature will calm her fear and give her a different perspective on the situation.

Your client immediately reacts to enjoying the sunshine on her face but her change in demeanor is brief as she quickly says that she doesn't "want to waste time" and that the both of you "should get down to business" on "solving" her problem.

You say, "Would you be open to trying something different today? I would like to know on a scale of 1 to 10 how difficult this situation is for you."

Your client almost screams at you that it is a ten and then emotionally shuts down. You tell her you understand that this is a very difficult time for her. She must feel very angry and frustrated.

While your client is nodding, you say, "I would like you to imagine for a moment that it is 10 years from now and you are past this challenge and you are having a cup of coffee with a loving friend. What would you and this friend want to say to yourself about this difficult time?"

Your client starts to laugh and says, "Get over it. It's not a big deal."

You sit for a moment and say, "Is this really how you and your loving friend would respond?"

Your client says, "No. She would tell me that she has believed in me all along and that it just took way longer than I originally anticipated. She would tell me that I'm smart and beautiful and that I'm too hard on myself."

You follow up with, "I wonder if you can treat yourself now the way in which you and your friend are treating you 10 years from now?"

Now your client is able to face her problem without running into her fear and frustration.

Tips for coaches

Most clients have an aha moment with this exercise. It demonstrates that they have the power to change the narrative in their head which leads to a decrease in fear and an increase in their ability to problem-solve. However, the resistance that comes from long-standing fear can be challenging and this exercise may need to be repeated as does the homework to engage in a joyful activity. Cultivating self-compassion skills takes time if it is naturally not a part of a person's normal way of acting. Continuing to identify how the client is compassionate toward others will help him or her develop the same skill for themselves.

POSITIVITY MINDSET HACK: HOW TO GO FROM DOUBT AND FEAR TO POSSIBILITY AND POSITIVITY

By Patricia Cimino

Positivity Mindset Hack takes your out of your fear zone and puts you in a place of excitement for what you could be creating in your life. It's for women with a professional background that are looking to discover their next chapter after they've finished raising their kids.

Great for:

- Women who want to return to the workforce but have lost confidence in themselves.
- Women deciding to start a business but afraid of taking the next step.
- Women struggling with self-doubt about which direction they should take.

– – –

Transitional times can be challenging because they require us to step out of our comfort zone and face the fear of stepping into a new, unfamiliar stage of our lives.

Many women go through a difficult transition in mid-life, when they are at the end of raising their kids and are looking to discover the next chapter of themselves. Often these women used to be professionals and then decided to leave work to raise their children and become the CEO of their household.

After years of raising her kids, this woman realizes that she would like to do "something" but has no idea what "something" is. She does know that she wants to make an impact in the world but doesn't want to go back to a cubicle or the corner office working 60 hours a week for someone else. This woman doesn't know what her possibilities are and is worried about making the wrong choice.

If you are a woman in midlife looking for a new direction, or just someone going through a transitional phase, this exercise will show you how your thoughts and beliefs can inspire you to take action or keep you in fear and doubt. This process will take the pressure off trying to be superficially "positive" by focusing on the "possibilities" instead. Exploring all the possible choices you have will give you an authentic positive energy so you can step into the next chapter of your life with clarity, confidence and optimism.

Steps

Step 1: Dreams and doubts
What would you like to do next with your life? For e.g. Do you want to start your own business, go back to university, apply for a new job or join a non-profit?

Write down everything you are thinking and believing about what you'd like to do and all the doubt and fear it's bringing up.

Step 2: Deep breathing
Close your eyes. Take 10 DEEP breaths, slow and full inhales and full exhales. Open your eyes.

Step 3: Possibility brainstorming
Write down all the positive possibilities of what could happen. Let your imagination go wild and expand your possibilities without limiting yourself. Time, money and age in this exercise are irrelevant.

Step 4: The power of possibility
Look at your answers in Step 1 and notice how they make you feel.

Write down a few notes about your feelings of doubt and fear.

Look at your answers in Step 3 and notice how they make you feel. Write down a few notes about your feelings of possibility.

This step shows you exactly how the power of what you are thinking and believing is causing you to feel. How you feel will drive what you do.

Step 5: Inspired Action
Create a list of possible next steps to move you forward and start to take inspired action toward each step written.

Case Study
One of my clients (like the many that I've coached) put her profession on hold to be at home with her kids. As her children got older, she knew there was something beyond motherhood for her to do. She felt a deep calling to do something more with her life.

Through the discovery phase of coaching she realized she wanted to be her own boss. She wrote down all the fears that came up around the idea of starting her own business and noticed that her thoughts and feelings spiraled downward because she had a lot of "I don't know" doubts.

When she allowed herself to write from a "what if..." scenario, she got super excited about the possibilities of what could be. Noticing on paper the feeling she got from reading the limiting beliefs compared to the "what if" list of possibilities, she realized her negative thinking were just thoughts that held no truth.

Today she is the proud partner/owner of a physical and occupational therapy business. Everything she described from her possibility list is embodied in her new business, from the design and decor of the clinic to the services offered to the exact clientele. She uses this tool when her business is faced with challenges and is able to move forward without letting the mind drama of doubts and fears take over.

Tips for coaches
Hold space for your client to think and feel both negative and positive emotions. This is instrumental because it allows them to experience both types of emotion and then choose what they want to do going forward.

REDEFINING SELF-WORTH: CHANGING YOUR MINDSET TO "I AM ENOUGH"

By Monica Devanand-Rajasagaram

This exercise helps women redefine their self-worth. It is for women who want to change the way they see and value themselves, so they can be confident in what they choose to do and be good role models for those they influence, including their kids, family and friends.

Great for:

- Women who are making life or career changes and worry about what others may think of them.
- Women who feel unhappy and frustrated in their current way of life, and feel stuck in moving forward in life.
- Mums who feel they have lost their value as a career woman because they choose to stay at home with their kids

— — —

Women go through many different phases in life – single life, career development, marriage, mothering, divorce – that all bring their own unique challenges. Many women will find, at some point, that they struggle with their self-worth and not feeling good enough.

A lack of self-worth can affect a woman's everyday life in many ways. A woman used to working may struggle with the idea of staying home with her kids because she doesn't want to give up her career. A working mum may feel undervalued for all that she does at her job and for her family. A woman thinking of a career change may feel judged for not sticking with one path.

Women often feel pressured by expectations that they be the ideal mum, career woman, or have the right body image or external appearance to please other people. These pressures can make women feel like they are only valued if they achieve something that is seen as worthy by the society they live in. When women don't feel like they're living up to these high standards, their self-esteem drops and they start to feel like they're not good enough.

The solution is to help women redefine their self-worth on their own terms. When a woman feels "good enough", she will also feel valued, worthy and confident to perform in her roles, to the best of her ability, and to role model this to those around her.

If you are a life coach using this exercise, you can help your client understand where her feeling of "not good enough" has stemmed from, and to help her see how she can shift her mindset towards feeling valued and "good enough".

Steps

1. Define your idea of "good enough"
How do you define being "good enough"? What are some things that will help you feel "good enough"?

Example: Is your "good enough" a reflection of how much you earn? Or a job you have, family status, number of kids, or how well you parent.

2. Importance of being "good enough"
Why is being "good enough" important to you? Does this affect your everyday living, ability to function, or sense of being valued?

Example:
Do you feel valued for what you do at home?
Do you feel significant as a work colleague?
How do you feel about your self-image and confidence?

3. What are your positive traits?
List 5-10 positive personal traits you have. This will help you see worth in your traits rather than external things, like looks,

wealth and career achievements. Personal traits are not to be confused with the roles you play in life.

Example: Are you trustworthy? Reliable? Loyal? Are you someone who is always willing to help?

4. What's shaped your identity?
Explore how your identity has been shaped and influenced by other people, groups or your society. This will help you re-evaluate your idea of self-worth.

Write down your strongest memory of how your identity has been shaped. Do you have a religious background that gives you a strong sense of identity? What role does or has your family played in shaping your identity? Have you had any other positive or negative influencers in informing and shaping your sense of who you are?

5. Exploring your past
Revisit your past. Expectations placed in childhood can shape your identity; therefore it is vital for you to identify these.

Write down any negative words or events that you feel may have changed the way you view yourself. Have family or friends spoken negative words about you that have had a big influence in your life? Is there a significant event or situation in your life where you have been told you're "not good enough"?

6. The impact of feeling "not good enough"
It is important to know how feeling "not good enough" is impacting your life and also those around you.

Is feeling "not good enough" impacting your work and family life or relationships? And if so, how?

Do you feel it is stopping you from achieving things you would like to?

Do you feel the need to constantly please others or to constantly strive to achieve something else that's going to make you feel good?

7. Take positive action
What would you like to see change?
List 3-5 positive changes you would like to see happen. Be as specific as possible. It could be a new thought or approach towards something that has previously made you feel "not good enough".

Example: I want to pursue that job regardless of what others think I am capable of. I want to take up ballroom dancing by next month. I want to wear a dress to the upcoming dinner, without wondering what others will think of me.

8. Redefining self-worth
For you to see change, a shift must happen. You need to prioritize what is important to you in order to make this happen. You don't need to neglect everything else, but you must also find value in yourself in order to redefine your self-worth.

Facing your past, or any negative thoughts that shape your idea of not being "good enough" is extremely important as you go through this process. Not facing them will not only trip you up but you won't be able to achieve a sustainable change in your self-worth.

Tips for coaches
This exercise can be done by the client before a coaching session, with feedback afterwards, or done together in a session. It is important to get the client to be as honest as they can when doing this exercise, as it will help them understand the problem they wish to work on. It is also important to note that this exercise may be uncomfortable for the client, especially when talking about negative situations that they may have or currently are experiencing as a result of feeling "not good enough".

It should be explained to clients that this session will help them explore the issues that may have influenced their idea of self-worth, and will help them find ways to redefine their self-worth, in moving forward towards a positive change in mindset.

UNCONSCIOUS WORK WITH FEARS OF FAILURE, SUCCESS AND CHANGE

By Lee McKing

This exercise helps you overcome your fears of failure, success and change in order to succeed in life. It's especially good for entrepreneurs and business owners because such fears hold them back towards their success. It works for anyone who needs a shift or to start taking steps towards positive change.

Great for:

- Entrepreneurs facing difficulties starting a business
- Business owners who have suffered from hidden fears for a long time
- People who fear change yet seek a better life

_ _ _

Some of the biggest things holding a person back from achieving their dreams, goals and desires are these 3 fears: fear of failure, fear of success and fear of change.

While fear of failure and fear of change are both very common, many people also fear the extra demands and changes that come with success. For example, an introvert may find the extra attention of success to be very uncomfortable. Even with positive changes, people may be afraid of getting out of their familiar comfort zone and secretly prefer to stay in their safe bubble.

This exercise will help you (or your client) overcome these fears so you can achieve success and live fully. Here are the steps to complete:

1. Identify the fear of failure (or success or change) to see if you have it. If you do, you will feel the fear coming from somewhere in your body. Identify where it comes from and on a scale of 1 to 10, where 10 is really fearful and 1 is nothing, give it a rating.

2. Now focus on the fear and trusting your unconscious mind, allow it to be represented by a symbol. Once you've got a symbol, take it out of the body and take note of a few details about it – it's color, size, movement, how it feels, etc.
3. Ask the symbol, trusting your unconscious mind to give you the answer, "What is your positive intention (or purpose) for me?"

   a. Most people will get an answer. Ask this question to the symbol and let the symbol respond, "If you can give me <answer 1>, what else can you give me that's positive?" Get at least 3 positive answers.
   b. Some people might not get any answers. It could be that they do not trust themselves or their unconscious mind. Another option is to work through the fear of change first, as it might be holding the person back.
   c. Very rarely too, some people might get negative responses. Repeat the previous question and remind the symbol and unconscious mind to give a positive response.

Now give thank and ask this to the symbol, "Thank you for giving me <answer 1>, <answer 2> and <answer 3>, but the thing is, do you know you have been giving me the fear of failure instead (or success or change)? So can you change to something else to give me all the positive and none of the negative?" and then wait for the symbol to change 100% before the last step.

Ask for its positive intention or purpose again and once it's all good, take the new symbol back inside the body, returning it to where it came from originally.

Case study
I worked with a man who happened to have all 3 fears of failure, success and change. Some clients have 1, 2 or all 3 of these fears.

41

I asked him to identify the source or root of the fear. It was in his heart, the fear of failure. And it was a rating of about 9 or 10. (Step 1)

I asked him to focus on it and the symbol of an old copper coin, like from ancient China, appeared. It was in his chest, so I asked him to take it out of his chest and put it in front of him. (Steps 2 and 3)

I guided him to ask the symbol, "What is your positive intention for me?" and the symbol replied, "to fail" so I reminded him to ask for a positive answer. The symbol took a while (it's ok to wait) and finally replied, "Wealth". (Step 4c)

So I repeated, "If you can give me wealth, what else can you give me that's positive?" "Happiness," he replied.

"And if you can give me wealth, and happiness, what else can you give me that's positive?" "Success," he replied.

We have 3 positive answers so we go into Step 5. "Thank you for giving me wealth, happiness and success but the thing is, do you know you have been giving me the fear of failure instead? So can you change to something else to give me all the positive and none of the negative?"

The symbol started changing and finally became a pure clear diamond. It wanted happiness, success and freedom! A new positive quality appeared. And then I asked him to take this new symbol back into his body. (Step 6)
And then I repeated this process for his fear of success and fear of change.

Tips for coaches:

- You can do this exercise with eyes wide open or eyes closed.
- Be open with the symbols that come up and respect them. If a knife appears, it may be good or bad

depending on whether it represents the fear or after the transformation. Or a cross might appear but it is not necessarily religious.

- If there is any resistance from the client, just continue chatting with your client and build rapport. Ease into it and if, in the worse case scenario, nothing happens, then nothing happens.

MEMORY CLOSET TECHNIQUE: REPLACE UNWANTED BEHAVIORS AND FREE YOURSELF FROM GUILT

By Julia Melnova

The Memory Closet Technique is about living an extraordinary life and being able to reach out to your superpowers on demand. It helps you tap into your inner resources and bring out the best qualities that you need for a particular situation. This exercise is for anyone that wants to become free of guilt and blame about behavior patterns that are no longer serving them.

Great for:

- People who have unwanted behaviors such as overeating.
- People without the discipline to stick to healthy habits or positive behaviors.
- People who lack a quality they need to accomplish their goals.

– – –

So many people are lacking self-confidence these days. This leads to unwanted patterns of behavior that then lead to guilt and even more of the unwanted pattern of behavior. This then leads to even more guilt and, as a result, to even lower self-esteem.

We don't realize that low self-esteem is a result of our own judgments and the pressure we put on ourselves. Not only do we achieve less and become less productive, ultimately we develop low self-esteem that can create a wide spectrum of unfortunate events and experiences for us.

People usually blame themselves for their inability to control their behavior and as a result think they don't deserve this lifestyle, this job, this body and, ultimately, this life.

My life mission is to show people that they are enough and that they are able to reach positive inner states that will empower them and make them "super human" in their own way.

The Memory Closet Technique helps you to create a powerful inner identity that you can access on demand to feel more confident. So many people think their behavior is no longer serving them and yet they keep their old patterns and blame themselves. This exercise allows you to tap into your inner resources (or someone else's inner resources) and bring out your best qualities to help you effectively deal with the situation you are dealing with.

Step 1: Identify your current and desired state

1. Identify the problem state you are currently experiencing, e.g. shyness, lack of ideas, trouble concentrating at work. Find out when the problem occurred for the 1st time, in the past, by remembering in detail when the problem occurred, where and under what circumstances.
2. Identify the resourceful state that will serve the problem the best by realizing which state/mood would work to make this situation better, what qualities you would need to obtain to make sure you are capable of dealing with the situation. For example, you might need more confidence, concentration or creativity.

Step 2: Your wardrobe of resourceful "outfits"
Envision that you have a wardrobe with resourceful "outfits". These outfits allow you to obtain or enhance qualities you are lacking or you need to increase in order to complete a task or situation with ease and confidence. For example, a shy person might need an outfit of a superman, and a person who needs to enhance his creativity might want to try on Walt Disney's suit.

1. 'Anchor' the gesture for your wardrobe to become available to you by choosing one point on your body and tapping there with your finger. An anchor can be made anywhere and it is a good idea to avoid "beaten path" areas of the body such as knees, shoulders and hands (these parts of the body are usually highly accessible for others and may trigger unwanted anchors when they are not requested). Instead, look for uncommon spots on the body such as tip of the nose, between the eyebrows, or under the ear to set up an anchor there. Keep in mind that once the anchor is set you will be able to access it automatically without thinking and the effect will last all your life unless it is collapsed on purpose.

2. Envision an outfit with your desired resourceful state and put it on.

Step 3: Go back to the 1st time when you experienced the problem

1. Identify the timeline in space where your future/past is located by standing up and pointing it out. Keep in mind that for some people the future is located to their right and past to their left, but it could be the opposite. For some people the future is out in front and the past is to their back.

2. Wearing the resourceful outfit, step on the timeline and close your eyes. Go into the past to the 1st time the problem occurred.

3. Open your eyes when you've reached that first time. How do you feel having those resources available at that moment? (Check the anchor by pressing on the selected point on the body to make sure that by pressing the anchor the needed resources are triggered and become available).

Step 4: Go to the present moment wearing the resourceful "outfit"

1. Go back to the present moment wearing the same resourceful outfit. See how having that resource available changes the meaning of your problem and your ability to resolve it.

46

2. From the present moment, still wearing your resourceful outfit, look back and see how life has shifted for you. You are now a victor instead of a victim of your own thoughts and mind.

Step 5: Bring the resourceful "outfit" into the future

Imagine yourself in the future utilizing all the skills that you have acquired by wearing this outfit. See yourself 5, 10, 15 years into the future.

Case study

John had trouble concentrating at work and came to me for help and assistance to become more concentrated during his work hours. We discovered that he was very good at concentrating when he was playing golf so we used that as his new resourceful state.

John envisioned a wardrobe with a selection of "concentration" suits and I anchored John's finger for the wardrobe to be available at any time he needed it. John tried his golfing suit on and it made him feel more concentrated and sharp. He identified his timeline as the past being left and the future being right, and remembered the first time he lost concentration was because he was very bored at his job.

As soon as John remembered his first time of not being concentrated I asked him to open his eyes and recall how his feelings evolved once the concentration suit had become available to him. I walked John through his timeline and suggested to open his eyes in the present moment still utilizing his new skill set. He realized how having an ability to reach out to this enhanced state of concentration at any time would change his life. He started to look differently at his situation, after he became aware of his ability to choose to concentrate at any time.

Tips for coaches:

- Make sure your client has enough space to move freely back and forth and up and down
- Quiet place is recommended and the exercise should not be interrupted once started for best results.

PART 2: BODY AND LIFESTYLE

Breathing – Energy - Healthy habits

HAVENING TOUCH®: SHUTTING THE MIND-BODY STRESS RESPONSE

By Scott Tolchin

Havening Touch® is a tool that you can use to rapidly shift from a highly negative emotional state to an empowering, resourceful and creative state of being. It's for anyone who finds themselves stuck in a distressing state of fear, anxiety, sadness, worry, or anger.

Great for:

- People who regularly experience anxiety, sadness, worry or anger.
- People who suffer from phobias, panic attacks or PTSD.
- People who want a natural method for improving their mental and physical health.

– – –

When it comes to getting results in any area of life, the one universal thing that everyone will have to deal with at one point or another is the mind and body's reaction to fear and other stressful emotions, such as anxiety, worry, panic, sadness, anger, and rage. While we usually think of these emotions as negative, they really are not. They are primal stressors generated by the brain's stress response mechanism in an effort to protect us from danger and to ensure our survival.

The problem is that this stress-response may be easily triggered any time we even think about something fearful or dangerous. In an instant, we are thrown into a fight-flight-freeze mode. We feel emotionally and physically distressed and we lose access to our best cognitive, creative, and performance abilities.

Havening Touch® is a specific kind of touch that can move you past your worries and fears and instantly restore you to a state of calmness, clarity, creativity, and resourcefulness.

Havening Touch® works by shutting off your sympathetic nervous system stress response known as the fight-or-flight internal alarm system using your own hands to generate an electroceutical signal that the brain associates with a "mother's touch". With this technique you touch areas of your face and body that are the same areas that a newborn baby comes into contact with from its mother immediately after birth. These touches signal the baby's brain to let it know it is in a "safe haven" and that it is safe, loved, and not alone. The brain then generates delta waves and releases feel-good neurochemicals, such as GABA, serotonin, and oxytocin. Using this technique may free you from anxiety, anger, and fear so that you can get to work and create the life of your dreams.

How to apply Havening Touch®:

Havening Touch consists of caressing three main areas of your body: the upper arms, the hands, and the face. You are going to go through all of the steps with your eyes closed.

Step 1: Arm Havening
Start by taking your right hand across the front of your body and placing it on the top of your left shoulder. Then take your left hand across the front of your body and place it on top of your right shoulder. Now I'd like you to firmly but gently, and moderately slowly, slide both of your hands down the upper and outer sides of your arms to the tops of your elbows. The stroke is in the downward motion only.

Release your grip, bring both hands back up to their starting position placed on the tops of your shoulders and do another stroke down the upper and outer sides of your arms to the tops of elbows. Now take a few moments to continue Arm Havening. Adjust the pressure and speed that you are using so that it feels comforting and soothing.

Step 2: Hand Havening

Place both of your hands together palm to palm and fingers to fingers just in front of the middle of your body. Anywhere within the region of your stomach or your chest is good. Firmly but gently, and moderately slowly, move each hand in a circular motion while keeping your hands touching each other. Now take a few moments to continue Hand Havening. Adjust the pressure and speed that you are using so that it feels comforting and soothing to you.

Step 3: Face Havening

The stroke of Face Havening is very much like what you would do if you were rinsing off your face with some water. And the starting position is just like you would use if you were playing peekaboo. So place both of your hands on your face, the right hand on the right side of your face and the left hand on the left side of your face. The pads of your fingertips should be on your forehead, and your palms should be under your eyes on your cheeks. Gently and slowly slide both of your hands down the sides of your face using the whole front of your hands – fingers and palms, until your fingertips reach the bottom of your cheeks.

Lift your hands just off of your face and bring them back to the starting position like they would be if you were playing peekaboo, and then gently stroke the sides of your face in the downward direction until your fingertips get to the bottom of your cheeks. Take a few moments to continue Face Havening, and adjust the pressure and speed that you are using so that it feels comforting and soothing to you.

As you apply the technique you are helping to teach your brain to more finely distinguish between real danger and perceived danger. Over time this will result in your stress response not being so easily triggered by things that are not really a danger to you.

Step 4: Distraction
Applying Havening Touch after being startled or getting angry will work all by itself. But if you are stressing or worrying about something then you are still continuing to trigger your stress-response. In cases like these you need to take your mind off of the upsetting condition by distracting yourself as you apply Havening Touch. Make the distraction something that is a little difficult to do, for example, counting aloud backwards from forty to zero by 3's or reciting the alphabet backwards. You're just keeping your worrying thoughts away long enough for Havening Touch to take effect.

Step 5: Finishing
Stop Havening Touch, take a nice deep cleansing breath and open your eyes.

A Few Words of Caution
If you have been Havening for five or more minutes, make sure that you are feeling sharp and awake before you drive a car or do anything that requires care and attention. Finally, if you have been upset because someone has tried to harm you and you need to report what happened, do not use Havening Touch. You need to be able to report the facts just as they happened and generating all of those delta waves can affect that.

Watch a video of me demonstrating how to use Havening Touch: http://SuperfyYourLife.com/activate

Dr. Ronald A. Ruden, author of *When the Past Is Always Present: Emotional Traumatization, Causes, and Cures*, is the co-creator of Havening Techniques

4-7-8 BREATHING: FIND RELIEF FROM DEPRESSION AND ANXIETY

By Rick Sharpe

The 4-7-8 Breathing exercise provides fast and readily available relief from stressful situations brought on by depression and anxiety. It's for people who struggle to manage stressful situations brought on by their thoughts or their external environment.

Great for:

- People who struggle with stress, anxiety or depression.
- People who can't get out of a cycle of negative thinking.
- People who need a method for quick and easy relief they can do anywhere.

— — —

A certain amount of stress in our lives can be useful and has a positive effect on our daily routines. Stress can drive our motivations and desires as well as alerting us, consciously and unconsciously, to potential danger. A millennia ago, our stress hormones were naturally activated for our own survival. It's how the human race has managed to evolve over thousands of years. Our fight-or-flight response readily activated when danger appeared or was perceived to be in our vicinity. Once the real or perceived threat had passed, these hormones and chemicals abated and our bodies returned to normal.

Humans are the only species on the planet that can trigger stress hormones and chemicals in the body with a thought or series of inter-connective thoughts and emotions for lengthy periods of time. In our modern lives, we are bombarded by numerous stimuli inducing higher levels of stress which in turn can regularly flood our systems with fight-or-flight hormones and chemicals. The human body is not designed nor equipped for these lengthy periods of self-induced stress and keeping it out of balance this way affects our immune system and creates a vulnerable environment for disease.

Depression and anxiety are two stressors which can negatively affect us on a daily basis over weeks, months or years. A thought or negative event can lead to an emotion which, if held on to for days can lead to a bad mood. Dwelling on this negative event over months becomes a negative disposition and over years can turn into a personality trait.

When I was dealing with an extremely emotional personal breakup, my days were filled with the darker emotions associated with depression. Most days I would wallow in mythologizing a relationship that kept me in a recurring cycle of stress-inducing thoughts and emotions that did not serve me in any positive way. It was emotionally debilitating and physically painful (the pain centers in the body do not distinguish between emotional and physical pain). This darker part of my life was awash with confusion, uncertainty, fear and many days I used alcohol to numb these feelings only to have them return with a stronger vengeance the next day. Staying in that emotional hell was not an option and I needed to find a way out.

My journey to emotional wellness was paved with curiosity, exploration and learning. I discovered the world of mindfulness and the importance of meditative practices. One of the most important discoveries that helped me through my periods of depression was the benefits of conscious breathing – being super conscious of my breathing and how air entered my body, where it went and how it left.

Depression has its roots in dwelling on past events and we cannot make the past a better place no matter how deeply or often we go there. So when I felt my mind wandering into those darker thoughts and self-doubt, I knew those greedy little gremlins of the past would return to torture my existence in the present moment. The mind cannot be in two places at the same time so when I was focusing on my breath I couldn't be also thinking about those dark thoughts.

The 4-7-8 Breathing exercise proved very helpful, especially during those times my mind would wander in between daily tasks or moving from one place to another. It was at these times when I was most vulnerable to depressive and anxious thoughts building up inside me. When I had the presence of mind to recognize this, I used this exercise to keep me centered and focused in the present "now" moment.

The following exercise by Dr. Andrew Weil takes almost no time, and requires no equipment. It can be done in any position, seated, lying down or standing, and can be completed anywhere.

Steps

Place the tip of the tongue against the ridge of tissue just behind the upper front teeth, and keep it there through the entire exercise. Exhale through the mouth around the tongue. Try pursing the lips slightly if this seems awkward.

1. Exhale completely through the mouth, making a whoosh sound.
2. Close the mouth and inhale quietly through the nose to a mental count of four.
3. Hold the breath for a count of seven.
4. Exhale completely through the mouth, making a whoosh sound to a count of   eight. This is one breath.
5. Now inhale again and repeat the cycle three more times for a total of four breaths.

Always inhale quietly through the nose and exhale audibly through the mouth. The tip of the tongue stays in position the whole time. Exhalation takes twice as long as inhalation. The absolute time spent on each phase is not important; the ratio of 4:7:8 is important. If you have trouble holding your breath, you can speed the exercise up but keep to the ratio of 4:7:8 for the three phases.

Using this technique for anxiety or depression is beneficial because it is an "on demand" exercise. For those who struggle emotionally, the opportunities to engage it may be daily or even hourly. As you improve your emotional wellbeing and your ability to be self-aware of your own thoughts and emotions, you won't need to use it so often. When you have control over your thoughts, you will also have control over your emotions.

This exercise is something that you can use for the rest of your life when you encounter all those momentary and regular stressors such as traffic jams, tax forms, queues at the grocery store and other people having bad days. It's like having that little go-to assurance in your back pocket to help stress pass through your body, knowing everything will be OK on the other side.

Tips for coaches
It helps to have the client focus on the rise and fall of the chest or the sensation of air passing through the nostrils. Have the client notice when their mind wanders and have them just notice that this is happening and gently bring the attention back to the breath to stay focused in the moment.

CREATING A DAILY RITUAL

By Cassandra Gablier

This exercise helps you develop a basic daily practice to start your mornings feeling calm and centered. In one week you'll fine-tune a morning ritual that you can commit to everyday! It's for anyone who wants to navigate their life with more peacefulness.

Great for:

- People who want to begin a morning practice.
- People who struggle with stress and want to feel calmer during their day.
- People who feel scattered or emotional and need to get more centered.
- People who want to get in touch with their sacredness.

— — —

When we begin our day with intention through a morning ritual, it's easier to come back to that place of centeredness so we are supported during the normal ups and downs of daily life. This also creates a space for the depths of our souls to speak clearly to us, so we can remain on the truest path for ourselves in life. This intentional daily practice will connect you to your Breath, your Body, your Inner Voice, and the Silence that Brings You Home. Commit to fill up your cup each day, so you have more of yourself to give to the world around you.

Morning ritual practice
Commit yourself to 7 days of a morning practice. Beginning on a weekend or Monday morning may be easier than beginning in the middle of a workweek.

Rather than begin with a full hour the first day, you only need to commit 15 minutes. This slow integration allows you to ease into a daily ritual. A gradual increase in the time you spend in your sacred space will set you up for longer lasting success.

Day 1: Commit to 15 minutes for your morning practice. It helps to have a time you stick to every day so your practice becomes a normal routine. (E.g. I will wake up at 6am, go to the bathroom, brush my teeth, drink water, and begin my practice).

On Day 1 set up a sacred space where you will practice each day:

- Where in your home would most support you to be focused and relaxed?
- What objects might you feel called to have near you during your practice?
- What helps you feel grounded and centered?

Example: Choose a yoga mat or blanket for sitting on. Create a ritual box or altar, which may include essential oils, sage/ Palo Santo, crystals, pictures of an inspirational figure (Jesus/ Buddha/Gandi), pictures of loved ones, treasured objects, etc.

Day 2: Commit to 20 minutes for your practice. Return to your sacred space (or grab your ritual box and take it outside). Take a few minutes to settle into this new space.

Set an intention for your day. For e.g. *Today my intention is to breathe. Today my intention is to be present. Today my intention is to speak in a respectful way.*

Once you have your intention, tune into your breath. If you know any breathwork techniques, feel free to incorporate them into today's practice. If you are new to consciously breathing (yes, it's something we must practice!), begin by observing your natural breath. Then take an inhale through the nose for 4 counts and exhale out the nose for 4 counts. Continue this or increase to 5 or 6 counts each. Repeat until you are fully present with your breath.

Return to your intention for the day and repeat it to yourself three times. Step into your day with presence.

Day 3: Commit to 20 minutes for your practice. Return to your sacred space and follow Day 2 directions.

With a paper/pen or other art supplies, allow yourself time to write some affirmations for your day. These can be taken with you as reminders in your car/purse/wallet or you can hang them up around your home (on mirrors, refrigerator, walls). Examples include: *I love the life I am creating. I rejoice in great health and I love my body. Abundance flows easily to me. I am happy, healthy, and whole.*

Conclude your practice by returning to your intention for the day.

Day 4: Commit to 30 minutes for your practice. Return to your sacred space and follow Day 3 directions.

Allow yourself time to tune into your physical body and decide if it would like stretching, yoga, dance, or strength training. (There are plenty of free short videos online if you need help with ideas.) Some days you may feel called for a strong practice while other days may require some gentle stretching and free flow movement.

Conclude your practice by returning to your intention for the day.

Day 5: Commit to 40 minutes for your practice. Return to your sacred space and follow Day 4 directions.

Spend at least 5 minutes making a list of things you are grateful for. You may use paper and pen or you may make your gratitude list mentally. If you are having a rough day, see if you can find the underlying beauty. For example, if you are in an argument with someone, perhaps find gratitude in the lessons you are learning on how to appropriately communicate your feelings and how to listen to another express their feelings.

Conclude your practice by returning to your intention for the day.

Day 6: Commit to 50 minutes for your practice. Return to your sacred space and follow Day 5 directions.

Find an easy sitting position and allow yourself to go inward into prayer. If you have never had a strong connection to prayer, a good place to start is with your gratitude list. Perhaps you have people you would like to pray for, or maybe it's you who needs to ask for support or direction. Regardless of your personal beliefs, this is a practice that meets you where you are and reaches out to that which is greater than all of us. Any form of prayer is perfect for you in this very moment.

Conclude your practice by returning to your intention for the day.

Day 7: Commit to 60 minutes for your practice. Return to your sacred space and follow Day 6 directions.

Remain in a comfortable seated position and take at least 10 minutes to sit in meditation. A great place to begin is by returning to your breath. There is no wrong or right way to meditate. Some people like to meditate with their eyes closed, while others prefer to have them slightly open. Allow the space for your thoughts to come and easily go while you become the observer of the experience. There are plenty of beginner guided meditations online that are great places to begin.

Conclude your practice by returning to your intention for the day.

Tips:

- Commit to at least ten minutes to start your day. Once you enter your sacred space, you are more likely to be there for longer than 10 minutes.
- Parents: Try committing to one of the seven parts each day (Monday Meditate, Tuesday Body Movement, etc.)

You can find more resources to create your morning ritual here: https://actualizedaffinity.com/create-a-morning-ritual/

BREATHING FOR ENDURANCE

By Kathy Hammonds

This exercise helps you increase your endurance by teaching you two techniques for improving your breathing technique. Most of us don't breathe correctly and this affects our mental and physical health. This exercise is for athletes, asthmatics, folks with sleep apnea, and anyone looking for more energy and endurance.

Great for:

- Improving athletic performance and physical stamina.
- Improving mental focus, clarity and mood.
- People who experience brain fog, fatigue or chronic health issues.

Our most vital nutrient is oxygen. We can go weeks without eating food and days without water, but without oxygen we are gone in minutes. Most of us don't use oxygen in an optimal way and we take this vital nutrient for granted. A significant majority of people over-breathe, taking in too much volume of air and breathing too frequently, from the upper chest. This maladaptive pattern disrupts the nervous system and slowly wreaks havoc on health and energy.

This exercise will train you to breathe more efficiently, to improve your endurance and your overall health. Clients find that practicing these simple steps regularly shifts their mood, energy, vitality and even their weight in a positive direction very quickly.

Step 1: Check your breathing patterns

First, check to see if you have any maladaptive breathing patterns.

1. Notice your breath right now. Are you breathing through your mouth or your nose?

Now, place one hand on your chest and one hand on your abdomen, close your eyes and breathe normally.

2. On your inhale, is your chest or your belly expanding?

3. Now notice (without changing anything) if you are completing your inhales? Your exhales?

4. After breathing for a period of time, do you notice an urge to yawn or gasp for air?

Now that you've completed your evaluation, let's describe the basics of proper breathing:

- Breathing should be in and out through the nose regardless of activity. The only exception is during strong exertion when it is proper to exhale through pursed lips.

- While inhaling, the lower ribs and abdomen should expand three-dimensionally. Breathing should not be just inflating the chest.

- Breathing should feel relaxed and complete. At the completion of your exhale, you should feel a sense of ease and calm.
- Yawning and gasping is a sign of over-breathing. This means you are taking in too much air.

If you identify any maladaptive breathing patterns, it is *vital* for you to correct those patterns. Practice slow, steady, diaphragmatic, nostril breathing every time it occurs to you, several times per day. You'll notice that your energy will become more calm and relaxed, and you'll feel more alert as a result.

Once proper breathing is established, the next step is to breathe less. Why? When we breathe too frequently and with more volume than we need, we expel greater amounts of carbon dioxide, lowering the blood levels of this gas. Low levels of carbon dioxide in the blood prevent oxygen from being utilized by the body in an efficient way. Fast and frequent breathing, beyond your current needs, deprives your cells of oxygen and results in fatigue, brain fog, lack of energy and low endurance.

Therefore, you need to train yourself to breathe:

- Correctly,
- With less volume, and
- Less frequently.

Before you begin training yourself to breathe less, it is important to measure your current CO_2 (carbon dioxide) tolerance.

Step 2: Test your CO_2 tolerance

Start by measuring your current CO_2 tolerance. We will be indirectly measuring the blood volume of CO_2 you can tolerate before your body signals the need to inhale. This is a fancy way of saying how long you can hold your breath comfortably.

1. Take a few rounds of normal breath through your nose.
2. When you're ready, exhale as you normally would and plug your nose.
3. Time how long it takes to get the natural signal to inhale.

This is not a competition to see how long you can hold your breath. It is a measurement to see when your body is asking for more oxygen, so be sure to measure the first urge to inhale. Your first inhale should not feel like a gasping for air. It should feel like a normal breath.

Gradually, you will want to build up to comfortably holding your breath for 40 seconds or longer. Improving your tolerance for CO_2 translates into greater endurance. The next exercise will help you to achieve that.

Step 3: The Square Breath

Set a timer or cadence counter or simply keep a rhythm by tapping your hand on your lap.

1. Inhale gently for 4 counts
2. Hold your breath for 4 counts
3. Exhale your breath for 4 counts
4. Suspend your breath for 4 counts.

Do several rounds of this square breathing exercise. Once you can do 15 rounds without feeling out of breath, increase the count to 5, then 6, then 7 and so on.

Square breathing is a great way to improve oxygenation of every cell in your body by increasing your CO_2 tolerance. You will feel the benefit right away. Once you get above a 10 count for 15 or more rounds, you are well on your way to having significantly greater endurance and energy.

Tips for coaches
First, walk your client through the practice of observing their breathing tendencies or simply observe them to determine if they are a mouth breather or an over breather.
Then, test their CO_2 tolerance. Once you have a baseline, you can measure your client's progress objectively.

Next, lead them through the square breathing process. Be sure to do at least 8 rounds with them. If they are very unfit drop the countdown to 2 or 3 per action. Assign square breathing as homework. Be specific about count, number, and repetitions.

Finally, assign square breathing as your client is engaged in activity. Walking or running is best because you can use their step cadence to count. Challenge them to maintain a long, slow, and steady square breath and gradually lengthen each phase of breathing. Practicing square breathing during exertion is a fantastic way to improve endurance quickly and efficiently.

SELF-MASSAGE: RELAX AND RENEW YOUR BODY, MIND, AND SPIRIT IN 7 SIMPLE STEPS

By Laura Hardy

Self Massage helps you become aware of any changes in your body, boosts your immune function and keeps you feeling and looking young. It's for people who are predisposed to cancer, suffer from autoimmune conditions or just want to improve their energy levels and general health.

Great for:

- People that have cancer or are predisposed to cancer
- People that suffer from fatigue or low energy
- People with autoimmune conditions
- Anyone wanting to improve their health and energy levels

— — —

Massaging your whole body everyday encourages the blood and chi (energy) to stay open and flowing, which improves your overall health. It improves cardiovascular health, decreases stress levels, improves immune function and prevents cancer. Self-massage also calms your nervous system, which helps you relax and leads to better, deeper sleep. It also helps to detoxify your body and maintain a healthy weight.

Using this simple self-massage technique will enable you to get to know your body deeply, be in charge of your own health, and be in tune with any changes that arise.

This technique includes breast massage, which is a wonderful preventive for breast cancer. Massaging the breasts improves lymphatic flow by stimulating the lymphatic system, which consists of a large network of vessels throughout the body that helps purify the blood and improve immune function. We are told to do our own breast exams, but this practice will help you know your breasts even better and notice if there are any changes. Breast massage will help keep your breasts supple and resilient while also increasing your immune system.

Self-Massage should be done at least 5 times a week. Performing this ritual will rejuvenate your body and mind, keep energy flowing throughout your body, detoxify your body's largest organ (the skin) and keep you feeling and looking youthful and nurtured.

Answer these simple questions before you start the self-massage practice and then reassess in a month to see how you have improved.

On a scale of 1-10 (1 being very poor and 10 being excellent), answer the following questions:

1. How would you rate your immune system (that protects you from getting sick)?
2. How would you rate the natural moisture of your skin (before you use moisturizer)?
3. How would you rate your energy levels?
4. How would you rate your health overall?

Self-Massage Steps:

1. Warm about a tablespoon of oil in your hands. Drip a good quality oil onto your hands, preferably organic olive oil, and rub your hands together until you feel them warming the oil.
2. With a flat oiled hand start at the top of your feet going up your legs with long strokes towards your heart. Repeat this as many times as you like, I would suggest at least 5 strokes per area. Every human body is different, so use a pressure that works for you. Continue on over your buttocks and your lower and upper back (as far as you can reach) with long strokes toward the heart.

3. After you finish with your legs, back, and buttocks move to your abdomen. Using fingertips and flat oiled hands start at the belly button and go in a circular clockwise pattern until the circle expands to your rib cage, ending on the left side of your abdomen and going down towards the left side of the groin.
4. Move to the breasts, begin with the right or left breast going in a circular pattern starting around the nipple and gradually expand your circles till you reach the armpit. Then change your direction and repeat the step above. End with gently massaging towards the armpit.
5. Move on to the tops of your hands and forearms gently stroking up towards your shoulder and neck, repeat on the other side.
6. If desired you can also do a quick facial and scalp massage. Place both hands on your head and gently move fingers through your scalp all over your head. Make small circular motions all over your face.
7. End with the soles of your feet. Gently stroke up from the heel of the foot to the toes, repeating as much as you desire. Finish with small circular strokes all over your foot.

You will feel younger and healthier following these steps at least 5 times a week. You will notice great improvements, especially with your energy levels almost immediately, and you will start to feel in charge of your own health.

THE ENERGY BALANCE METHOD

By Joey Romeu

The Energy Balance Method helps you increase your daily energy, focus and results, while helping you balance your lifestyle. It shows you how to be consistent with the right habits, so you can perform when you need to without feeling drained. It's for coaches, entrepreneurs, busy professionals and anyone who wants better health, productivity, energy and overall fulfillment.

Great for:

- People who are having trouble with focus and procrastination
- People who are struggling with motivation crashes and overwhelm
- People who want more energy and less stress
- People who want to be more effective and achieve their goals faster

---

One of the biggest problems people face when running a business, bringing up a family, or progressing their career is stress. It drains us of energy, and when it isn't managed in the right way, it can make us sick, overweight and depressed. Day-to-day this can show up with feelings of guilt and overwhelm. We then distract ourselves, procrastinate and sabotage our results or give up.

There are many factors that affect our energy, including digestion, our environment, and our thoughts. When we do things we love that stimulate our creativity and focus, this energizes our body and makes us feel alive. When our minds are cluttered, we treat our bodies badly and have unhealthy relationships, which can drain our energy.

The key to overcoming this is to first get clarity on where your energy is being wasted, and what you could focus on instead to feel more vibrant and alive. The next step is to prioritize and track your habits consistently. Around 20% of your habits and efforts drive 80% of your results in any area of your life. Likewise, 20% of your habits and efforts will also drain 80% of your energy, or prevent 80% of your results. When we know what habits to focus on and where to direct our energy, we can have exponential growth and results by focusing only on things that drive results and fulfillment.

It is also important to choose healthy habits. The right balance of eating and exercise will also give you more energy. Drinking enough water (e.g. 1-3L daily) and eating plenty of fats during the day, rather than relying on sugar or stimulants, will give you far more consistent energy without the crashes. Meditation, gratitude and journaling are also powerful practices that energize and improve your focus.

If you are a busy entrepreneur, parent or professional, this exercise provides the foundation for increasing your energy and building powerful habits so you can get things done faster, improve your results and progress in any area of your life, while feeling happier and more fulfilled.

Step 1: Drain vs. Gain

1. Draw a line down a piece of paper, and on the left write "Drain", and on the right write "Gain".
2. On the left side of the page write down all the things you do day-to-day that drain you of energy, and anything you do regularly that you don't enjoy doing, things that stress you out, make you feel worse or don't serve you.
3. On the right side, write down things that you enjoy doing and give you energy, make you feel more alive and make you feel confident, accomplished or fulfilled.
4. Decide on one thing you will do more of that will give you more energy (from your Gain list), and the one thing you will focus on reducing that drains you of energy (from your Drain list). Note: What's the balance of time spent in each of the two areas?

Step 2: Habit Tracker

5. Think of a specific outcome or vision you want to achieve. For example, if it was related to health and fitness, this could be the outcome of you being in perfect health, with a swimmer's physique, and being free from pain. If related to business, it could be to run a successful business doing what you're passionate about.
6. Create a habit tracker by getting a blank weekly calendar, finding a blank week in a diary, or getting a piece of paper and drawing a table landscape with Monday to Sunday across the top. Down the left-hand side, create 5 new rows. *Alternatively, you can print a copy of a weekly habit tracker at https:// doubleyourenergy.co/p/habittracker).*
7. Decide on the 3-5 habits that will best serve you in reaching your specific outcome or vision that will make the biggest difference to your results right now. You can also add in the one thing that you will do more of that will give you more energy that you decided in part 1 (Drain vs. Gain).

Here are some examples for health and fitness:

- Drink 2.5L water daily.
- Sleep 7-8 hours.
- Eat a healthy breakfast high in protein and fibre.
- Eat 2 healthy meals a day.
- 15-30 minutes workout.
- Stretching, Yoga or Pilates.

8. Make your habits specific, and decide on whether you will do each habit daily or a specific number of times each week. Make sure the changes are small so that you feel at least 80-90% confident you can achieve them. Write them in your new habit tracker in the 5 rows you created in step 6.
9. Stick the habit tracker on your fridge, or on the wall in your room, office or somewhere you will see it regularly,

and put a tick or a cross on which habits you did or didn't do at the end of each day.
10. After 7 days review your week (e.g. How was your energy and performance? What went well? What didn't? What was the impact of not doing certain habits? What will you do more or less of? What will you start or stop doing? What's your number one focus for next week?)

You can use this habit tracking tool to find out what you love doing, what you're great at, what slows your results and what drains you. You can use it to review your progress and figure out what is or isn't working, so you can decide what the most effective actions to take are and adjust your plan to make it work best for you.

Tips for coaches
Using this exercise with a client can be beneficial to gain clarity on which areas of their life are most important to focus on, and it could be that there is more than one area they should focus on.

This exercise can be done individually by your client with your feedback in a coaching session, or done with you in a coaching session. Your client should aim to expand as much as possible on part 1, in order to figure out what lights them up, what brings them down and where they are most effective so that they can then focus on that and progress each week.

If you or your client are not at least an 8/10 or a 9/10 confident that they can achieve the decided goal for each habit, make the habit easier, or the change smaller.

THE BREATH: OUR GREATEST ALLY

By Kelly Biasiolli

This exercise helps you tap in to the present moment so you can recognize what's going on in your body, mind, and heart, and then act from that awareness. It's particularly useful for people making decisions, trying to listen to their intuition, engaging in challenging conversations/activities, or those experiencing frenzied or chaotic energy in the environment around them.

Great for:

- People dealing with chronic mental chatter or emotional triggers.
- People suppressing stress, doubt, indecision or fear.
- People who are challenged by interactions with coworkers, friends or family.
- People who desire greater peace of mind, calm, or sense of self.

– – –

The breath – it is subtle, it is constant, and it is always with us. As the single most involuntary, consistent and essential mechanism in our lives, it has powerful potential to be our greatest tool, ally, gift and indicator of what is going on for us physically, mentally, emotionally and spiritually, in any given moment.

I regularly work with people by using high impact activities, such as rock climbing, rappelling, and high ropes courses to create opportunities for personal transformation and growth. The reminder to *"breathe"* is the most common suggestion and support offered by one's partner or teammates, and for good reason.

The breath not only brings vital oxygen to all parts of our body (including our brain), which is helpful to have when you are

45 feet off the ground, gripped or trembling uncontrollably, but it's also a gateway to our nervous system. Each exhale activates the parasympathetic nervous system, which is the relaxation response in the body. Each inhale activates the sympathetic nervous system, which prepares the body for action: fight or flight. We must inhale to be able to exhale, so both responses are obviously necessary for the body, though the attention we give to quality and details of each is the true gateway to utilizing the breath to bring us greater awareness and control.

Over the years I have found it helpful to emphasize the *exhale* when coaching people in these high impact environments, as it naturally relaxes us and offers a moment to pause, become aware and choose how to respond, versus instantly react. It can also offer an interruption to thought patterns that may or may not be serving us.

When I am climbing and I come upon a move that seems improbable, scary or otherwise of high consequence, I pause long enough to fully exhale – out my fingertips, toes and even my face. Sometimes it requires a longer pause and deliberation about the next move. Often though, fully exhaling can bring such acute awareness and a moment to relax the parts of the body that don't have to be engaged – scrunched shoulders, clenched jaw, squinting eyes, and tensed calves. This not only saves energy, but allows for softness in the body that can translate to openness, space and calm in the mind.

Undoubtedly, this holds true for everyday moments. How we respond to challenge in any environment can offer clues to how we habitually respond to our daily challenges.

A good way to gain insight into how awareness of the breath can be useful in your daily life is to commit to studying it.

The Exercise

1. For 1 day, set the intention to bring awareness back to your breath as often as possible. Be an observer and see what you notice:

> • Do you ever hold your breath during the day? If so, when, why, for how long? This might be indicated with a big sigh that occurs once you've finally started breathing again.
> • Do you sigh loudly or for great length?
> • Is your breathing ever shallow?
> • Do you ever feel out of breath or as though you can't catch your breath (aside from when you're doing aerobic activities)?

2. After several days of basic observations, experiment with the following:

> • What happens in the rest of your body and mind when you become still (sitting or standing) and you bring complete focus to the tiny pause that exists between the in-breath and the out-breath?
> • What do you notice if you count your inhale and exhale?
> • Do the numbers match up?
> • Which parts of your torso move (stomach, ribs, chest, collarbone)?
> • What happens to the rest of your body after watching several sequences of counting in and counting out?

These tasks can be done nearly any time of day – simply standing still, sitting at a stop light, waiting in line, on a break, while sitting on a park bench, before addressing a group, or before falling asleep.

3. As you begin to develop more awareness of your natural breathing tendencies, as well as observations with counting

and pausing, deliberately bring some regularity to your observing.

- Set a time each day to observe the pause between the exhale and inhale. Any time can work as long as you can commit to being fully present for 15 or more seconds.

In the beginning, the point is not necessarily to change the breath (unless that feels necessary); it is simply to notice. Being the watcher can lead to all kinds of insight around our most basic and essential bodily function, which, in turn, can be our greatest tool.

In practicing breath awareness you may notice how you unknowingly hold your breath, particularly in challenging moments or times of uncertainty. This has been the case for many of my clients that needed to make a decision – even the most basic decision, while preoccupied or in an unsettling environment. Once the decision was made, they let out a noticeable exhale that then cued them to recognize the increasing tension that was growing in their body while they stopped breathing for a short time.

To help remedy this tendency, they took a deep, full breath in and out before making any decisions. Not surprisingly, they found that practicing with less significant matters such as deciding which ice cream flavor to choose at the store (*which is not necessarily a trivial thing*), increasingly developed their awareness, thereby training the breath to help them make pivotal decisions down the road.

Tips for coaches
This exercise can be utilized by anyone at any stage in their development. Some clients may have a tendency to qualify what they're experiencing as a "right or wrong way to breathe". At this stage in the game, you can best help them be diligent about observing consistently (perhaps multiple times a day for a week) before trying to change or *fix* anything. It can be helpful to break things down to just one focus a day. Let this be easy.

FEELING HOT! HOT! HOT! REBALANCING YOUR FIRE ELEMENT

By Danielle Sangita Rottenberg

This exercise helps you bring your body and mind back into balance naturally. It's a simple and easy way to determine if you are experiencing signs of burnout or have too much fire in your system. This exercise offers lifestyle, dietary and meditation tips for anyone that is feeling overstressed, agitated, or angry.

Great for:

- Anyone that has a high stress job, including corporate professionals, lawyers and doctors.
- People who are experiencing agitation, anger, insomnia or a racing mind.
- People who can't laugh or enjoy life because they are so focused on their work, finances, to-do list, etc.

- - -

In our modern world many people are constantly pushing themselves in every direction: at work, home, with family obligations, in an effort to reach personal and professional achievements. We are burning out at a rapid rate. We have become a society of constantly doing!

Fatigue, lack of energy, a reduction in motivation, tension and the inability to enjoy everyday life can be signs that you too are suffering from stress-induced burnout. People who take on way too many projects, who have a to-do list that is two pages long, who work excessive amounts of hours each week, who rarely say no to requests are at higher risk of burning out. They need self-care to balance out their stressful way of living but are the least likely people to make time for it. They also tend to like the adrenaline rush of working, being overstimulated and pushing their mind and body to new limits.

This full steam ahead approach can cause the mind to become "fiery" or "overheated". We then become incapable of turning off our to-do list in our minds, while becoming more and more detached from our true nature.

This exercise is based on the principles of Ayurveda or "the knowledge of life", centered on the 5 elements; Fire, Air, Water, Earth and Ether/Space. Ayurveda focuses on keeping these elements in balance in order to create the harmony needed for good health. In this instance, burnout is a case of having too much "Pitta" or Fire/Water element. Often times when the Fire/Water element is out of balance, these individuals are already overextended. Their "can do" attitude and nonstop pace will surely wear out their adrenals, which are producing cortisol at high rates just to keep up.

Here are just a few possible signs that you have too much fire in your system: criticism of yourself and of others, being overly judgmental, feeling short-fused or impatient, being fiercely competitive or argumentative, assuming you are always right and being described as having an intense personality. Notice how these traits all contain a fiery element? These traits are highly celebrated in our culture, actually imperative to success many would say! To some degree, a fiery nature is helpful, but finding the right balance is fundamental.

In this exercise we will be focusing on the Fire element, as fire is related to burning out. If any of these Fire patterns sound familiar to you then it might be time to look at cooling that fire by bringing in food, herbs, breath work, yoga, meditation, aromatherapy or guided imagery.
This exercise will help you identify if you have a fiery mind and what you can do to balance it.

Use this checklist to rate yourself:

1 is No, not at all
3 is Sómetimes
5 is a strong Yes

81

1. Are you competitive?
2. Are you critical of yourself?
3. Are you critical of others?
4. Do you push your mind and your body to unhealthy limits?
5. Are you argumentative (always trying to make your point)?
6. Do people say you are intense or too serious?
7. Are you impatient or short fused?
8. Do you experience acid reflux or heartburn?
9. Do you break out in acne, boils or rashes?
10. Do you get up in the middle of the night and have a hard time going back to sleep?
11. Is it hard for you to turn off your brain, like it is on a hamster wheel?
12. Do you often get up around 2 or 3 am and have a hard time falling back asleep?

If the majority of your answers fall in the 4 to 5 range, then here are some great tips for bringing your fiery mind back into balance.

Diet

- Eat more cooling foods such as cucumbers, melons, grapes, coconut and coconut water, avocados, pomegranates. Add asparagus, sweet potatoes, green leafy vegetables, and pumpkin seeds to your diet. Chose spices like cilantro, cardamom, fennel and coriander to your dishes.
- Decrease (or remove) your intake of fiery foods like spicy Thai food, hot sauces on Mexican dishes, or hot Indian curries.
- Monitor or reduce alcohol intake, as this can cause extra heat in your body.
- Try switching from that 2nd or 3rd cup of coffee a day to a mint or chamomile tea.

Lifestyle

- Allow free time every day. Enjoy the beauty of nature. The blueness of the ocean or the incredible lushness of the forest; these colors are especially great for "cooling the mind".
- Turn off that cell phone, computer, and television an hour before bed. We need to decompress before sleeping and it is crucial to activating the parasympathetic nervous system. If we are tied to that constant barrage of "doing-ness" all day and night our body cannot get into "rest and relax" mode.
- Use rose, lavender, peppermint, or sandalwood essential oils in your aromatherapy diffuser at work or at home.

Meditation, yoga and breathwork

- Sit in stillness or meditate at least 15 minutes a day. Guided imagery is a wonderful tool for an overactive and overstimulated mind.
- Create a cool yoga practice: standing forward folds, cobra pose, moon salutations, and twists, at a slow-flow pace. Limit hot yoga or Ashtanga styles, for that heightens heat in the body and the mind, and also encourages our competitive nature.
- Use alternate nostril breathing as part of your breathwork or just take deep long exhales, like that big old much needed SIGH, which is great for releasing heat.

Tips for coaches:
We can all benefit from checking in with ourselves and our clients. Add this to your evaluation process. Many times we are working only with the physical body. The mind and spirit are equally important to health.

THE ART OF TRANSPARENCY: USING VULNERABILITY TO CREATE LASTING CHANGE

By Mike Ratliff

This exercise helps you break through mental barriers that hold you back from making positive changes to your health. It helps you discover your deeper motivation for change and learn to accept help so you can commit to lasting improvement for your health journey. This exercise is for anyone that struggles with poor health or wants to improve their health.

Great for:

- People struggling to commit to their health goals around weight loss, healthy eating or quitting smoking.
- People who backslide after making good progress on their health goals.
- People who want to make lasting changes to their health.

– – –

"Honesty and transparency make you vulnerable. Be honest and transparent anyway."
--Mother Teresa

I have found for a person to make a lasting change, they must first figure out how they got to where they are currently. They must discover why they are willing to make a change. They must work out the roadblocks that are keeping them away from their goals.

This exercise is designed to help breakthrough your roadblocks to better health by helping you identify your motivation for making changes and learn how to be transparent and vulnerable with yourself so that you can open up and let others in to help. The key is to dig deep and be real and honest with yourself...about the good and the bad!

I have used the art of being transparent in our business for 6 years as we help people reach their health goals through personal coaching. When we work with people we ask open-ended questions to help people think through why they chose this time to make a change in their health journey and how it would benefit them and the people in their lives. I have found that people respond to and are more motivated by "real life, vulnerable" stories over facts. Through discussions and telling stories about our own journeys or the journeys of others, we really dig down and make important breakthroughs that inspire people to commit to positive change in their own lives.

Step 1: Get clear on your Why

1. What brings you to this decision to make a change in your health journey?

Think about why you made the decision to make a change or seek help to begin with. What has been going on in your life that caused this decision?

I often hear people say that they had that one "aha" moment where they decided that enough was enough. It isn't until we stumble on that road block a couple (or a couple hundred) times that we decide that we are "sick and tired of being sick and tired." Only at this moment are we willing to make a change.

2. What people in your life would benefit, if you were able to do more and be around longer? How would they benefit?

Think deeper about why you would want to be consistent and complete your goal for the people you love. This can create a stronger motivation for staying on track with your health. Are you a grandparent that wants to be able to get down on the floor and play with your grandkids? Are you a parent that wants to be able to keep up with your kids?

3. What benefits will YOU have if you reach your goal?

Think about all the things you will be able to do by reaching your goal. This might include having more energy to play sport, being able to travel or ticking something off your bucket list. Some people have even told us that the benefit would be proving to themselves that they can have a thought, design a plan and then stick to it.

Make a list, including how you will feel and what new things you will be able to accomplish. Post this list where you can see it everyday. This will help you remember why you are doing what you are doing!

Step 2: Accept help from others

We have found that when a person is ready to make a change in their health journey, it is better to get help from someone that has been on that journey already. Most health and wellness coaches became coaches because they found success on their own journeys and then wanted to help others achieve the same. When you are really honest with yourself about your health and what's holding you back, you will be vulnerable enough to accept help from a coach.

What are you willing to change to be vulnerable and accept help from others?

Again, make a list of what you want to change. Examples: The amount of times that you will be contacting your coach or personal trainer. Reaching out to your coach when you're stuck. Being honest about your health habits with your family. Clearing things off of your "mental plate" and asking for help with daily tasks so you have more time to spend on your health.

Use post it notes posted where you will see them during your day to remind you of your goals and promises to yourself.

Case Study

Here is the story of how my brother Marty allowed himself to receive my help and achieved a lasting transformation in his health.

My brother struggled with his weight and he told me that everything that he had ever done in his life was a failure when it came to weight management. I explained that if he was ready, I could help him reach his goals. The key statement for him was: "if he was ready." I have found that if you talk someone into making their decision, you will always be talking them into working on their goals.

My brother proved that he was ready and even said that he would prove me wrong by being my only failure. I accepted the challenge and we began to work towards his goals together. We stayed in close contact each day (sometimes multiple times per day) as he was navigating through the many changes that he was making.

Month after month, Marty was transparent and vulnerable with me about what was happening in his body and in his mind. It was his ability to be honest with his feelings that allowed him to be successful. Over a period of 9 months, Marty was able to lose 105 pounds while maintaining his health. His doctor was stunned when he showed up 105 pounds lighter and not on the verge of Type II Diabetes and High Blood Pressure. It's been 6 years and Marty is still down 95 pounds.

Being vulnerable, honest and transparent with yourself really does open doors to allow breakthroughs. These breakthroughs are the direct result of allowing yourself to hear that little voice inside your head that tells you enough is enough. Only at that point will you take the first step, accept help and understand that you can start working on goals and a plan that you can commit to.

PART 3: HAPPINESS

Relationships – Values – Inner Wisdom

PRIORITIZE HAPPY: GET A HEALTHY WORK-LIFE BALANCE BY GIVING AS MUCH FOCUS TO LIFE AS YOU DO TO WORK

By Sarah Ross

Prioritize Happy helps you avoid chronic stress and burnout by learning how to regain balance in your life. It's time to rediscover what makes you smile! This exercise is for corporate executives and entrepreneurs who are constantly chasing the next big pay rise, job title or deal and have stopped making time for fun and enjoyment.

Great for:

- People feeling stuck or unhappy in their lives
- People burnt out from stress at work, constantly chasing that next pay-rise or promotion
- Anyone wanting to improve their Life-Work-Balance
- Anyone who needs to bring fun and laughter back into their life after a period of depression, illness or stress.

— — —

It is so easy to get caught up in the desire to keep achieving more and more that it takes over everything. Working late in the office, taking the laptop on vacations and not eating or sleeping properly all contribute to a state of burnout. "When this event is over" or "Once I've signed this deal" become the excuses to put off doing the very activities you need most such as spending time with family and friends, exercising and eating healthily. All of these activities help keep you in balance and allow you to reach your goals in an optimal way.

In order to do less to deliver more, you need to take time away from what's creating stress in your life. I was burnt out, stressed, and travelling 85% of the time, yet not even daily migraines were enough to make me stop and wonder if there was more to life. For me it took taking redundancy from the corporate world to give me the time to focus on what I really needed, and it wasn't more time in the office. Only once I started to put as much effort into my life as I did to my job, did I recharge and start to live again.

You need to recharge so that the time you actually spend working is as productive as it can be without taking over your whole life. It's time to prioritize being happy in the same way you would for an important meeting or work project.

This exercise helps you avoid burnout by re-establishing the balance in your life through reconnecting to activities that you no longer make time for. By prioritizing being happy, you experience quality time away from the stressful situations whilst allowing your body to rest and recover.

Steps

1. Write a list of everything that makes you happy
This list should include things you enjoy doing but don't have time for anymore, people you like hanging out with or simply your favorite things e.g. food, films, books. If it makes you laugh or smile thinking about it, put it on your list.

You may find it hard to think of anything as you haven't given them any time in your life for a while so use these questions to help you write your list:

- What did you love to do as a child?
- What's your favorite meal/activity to celebrate success?
- If money, time and resources were not obstacles, what would you spend the day doing?

As a child, I was a bookworm and always had my head in a book. Yet as an adult, during the worst of my own burnout, I stopped reading. I didn't even have books next to my bed anymore, and I certainly never went to bookshops. The day after I wrote my list, I went to a bookshop and walked out with four new books.

2. Commit to doing at least two of the activities on your list every day.

Make it interesting and do different things each day but make it a priority to do something completely non-work related every day. Schedule it into your day if you need to.

My calendar keeps me sane. If something is in the calendar, it gets done. Everything from morning to night for work was in my diary, yet I rarely scheduled anything non-work related. In fact, I would make my social life fit around work appointments. Once I started to schedule time to read, walk home or cook dinner, I actually started to make them as high a priority as my work assignments or trips.

Be sure to spend time away from your office, desk and the sofa. In fact, avoid anywhere that you tend to spend time when you are feeling low and stressed.

3. Make your list visible.
Think about where you will actually see your list every day. I have a copy on my fridge as well as in my phone. If I'm having a stressful day, I'll read through my list and choose something from it. Sometimes it's enough to just read through the list and remember how doing those activities makes me feel. Other times I need to go and do the activity I chose.

4. Keep adding to your list
As you find activities that make you smile and put that bounce back in your step, add them to your list. As I started to read more, I recalled that the best times I had when I was younger included eating an apple whilst reading a book, so that was added to the list.

Remember, a smile can change how you feel in an instant, so prioritizing happiness doesn't have to be a huge time commitment. In the beginning, it will take some effort to create the balance again in your life, but the more frequently you do it, the easier it becomes.

Tips for coaches

If your client is struggling to think of a list of things that they enjoy doing, ask them what they used to enjoy doing as a child. Often the things that made us smile and laugh as children are still powerful activities for us as adults.

Some clients may need to start with small steps, start by getting them to do a number of the activities over a week and build up to doing something every day.

THE ASSERTIVENESS COMPANION: LET ASSERTIVENESS CHANGE YOUR LIFE!

By Alessandra Patti

The Assertiveness Companion helps you communicate your needs to other people and say no to requests that you don't want to or can't do. It shows you how to use assertive language in your communication so you can say no while still respecting the other person. This exercise is for anyone that has difficulty saying no to requests or feels like they have to please others all the time.

Great for:

- People pleasers who struggle to say no.
- People who have suffered from burnout.
- People who take on too many tasks or responsibilities.

– – –

In our daily life the people around us, both at work and in our private lives, request things from us all the time. Not all requests are feasible or in line with our values and priorities.

However, in many cultures, saying NO to someone else's request is thought to be selfish. So sometimes saying YES but really wanting to say NO becomes the rule. When this becomes a pattern, other people's needs become locked into our subconscious mind as our priority over our own needs. Because of this habit, we might tend to say yes way too often and reduce our level of assertiveness when it comes to stating our own needs. I call it "the juggler syndrome" and I had it once too before I realized that what I was doing wasn't good for me. I was saying yes too often, even taking up things which were not my responsibility because I wanted to be accepted.

A juggler typically answers with "yes", "sure", "why not", and "of course" to requests that are clearly overwhelming or not manageable, like an impossible deadline from a boss, or those friends always asking to be driven somewhere, even when they can do it themselves. It is normal to want to please people we like. However, by always accepting these requests, enormous distress and resentment can grow inside the juggler. It can also lead to these other consequences:

- Poor time management: Because jugglers please everyone else first, time flies and they will struggle to get their own work and tasks finished. This then leads to stress and anxiety.
- Guilt: If self-care is considered selfishness in their culture or family circle, and therefore discouraged, jugglers might feel guilty for not taking care of others first. This guilt imprisons the jugglers by making them feel like they always have to say YES.
- Confusion about values and loss of personality: A juggler usually doesn't know his/her values. Because those values coincide with someone else's priorities, the juggler's personality gets lost. If the habit of following others' priorities becomes the rule, the juggler might lose perspective in what truly matters for him/her.
- Poor boundaries: Jugglers find it difficult to set boundaries and figure out what is an acceptable request and what is not. For example, if a boss gives you impossible tasks and you always say YES, the Moon becomes the limit. You keep doing things that aren't in your best interest and you might end up suffering from burnout.

The solution and the coaching technique!
You can overcome the issue of saying YES when you want to say NO. It is possible! Feel proud of taking this first step.

Step 1: Identify your YES pattern
Take a pen and paper and write down with absolute honesty:

1. Three situations where you have said YES during the last month, but you really wished you could have said NO. Observe, for at least 3 minutes, how those YES's made you feel.

Example: I was very tired and my friends knew it, but they insisted I drive them to that party. I stayed there until 3 am even though I didn't want to.

2. If you could have said NO, what would you have said? Write the exact words for each situation. This will help you *practice* the hint of a NO in preparation for being more assertive.

Example: I would have said: "Hey, I am very tired. I'm going home and we will party another day."

Step 2: Transform your language
The way we communicate what we want is a key to being more assertive. People might not always agree with our choices, but being assertive with our language will help establish a clear NO.

Example 1: Let's assume you wished to have said:
"No, I can't pick your friend up at the airport, since I have my dancing class at the same time".

What about transforming the sentence even more? Try this:

"I would be glad to help. However, I have my dancing class at the same time and this is like therapy to me. I cannot skip it this time. Thank you for understanding."
"I would be glad to help" = This shows your interest for the request.
"This is like therapy to me" = Here your logic for saying NO is undeniable and your need is expressed.
"Thank you for your understanding" = You ask the other person for compassion.

Example 2:
"I am sorry, I cannot do the presentation within 24 hours. I am missing data, but if you really want to, maybe I can do a draft."

Let's transform it:

"I can certainly make a draft of the presentation. However, the details missing will make it incomplete. Timing does not help either in making it outstanding. What about doing it for next week and have the complete data and the presentation polished?"

"What about doing it...?" = This suggestion shows your proactiveness towards the task.

Example 3:
"Sorry, my house is a mess right now. I cannot host the party even if you want to help me clean. Too stressful!" What about:

"You know I love throwing parties. I am quite tired this week, though. I would appreciate if you could consider doing it at yours. We can find another solution/location if not".

"I am quite tired...I would appreciate if you could consider doing it at yours." = This sentence establishes firm boundaries and you have no apologetic tone.

Step 3: Use assertive body language
If you're transforming your language in the steps above and other people still don't accept your NO, then go to your mirror and practice this assertive body language:

1. Torso up, arms relaxed.
2. Imagine looking at the other person in the eyes, in a natural way.
3. Clear your voice and let the words come out in a higher pitch than usual.
4. Speak out loud the sentences you created in step 2.

You can't control other people but you can control your body language.

Tips for coaches:
- At the beginning the client might resist Step 3 of the exercise, because it can be quite tough to role-play on their own. Suggest a role-play between the two of you.
- Encourage the client during the whole process, either when they do the exercise on their own or during the role-play.
- Have the client vocalize *every word* properly. Encourage eye contact.
- Repeat the process.
- Go deeper with the client. If your client is a juggler, they might try to please you too, and not practice on their own. Check progress on a weekly basis.

PERSONAL RESONANCE: MAKING DECISIONS FROM YOUR INNER WISDOM

By Lois and Julia Thompson

Personal Resonance assists you in making decisions by showing you how to identify what you vibrationally align with. Instead of analyzing your choices, this exercise helps you tune in to your body to get the answer. It's for anyone that is blocked making decisions, doesn't trust their own instincts or feels stuck from moving forward in their life.

Great for:

- Getting unstuck from limiting beliefs
- Making heart-centered decisions
- Helping clients learn how to validate their own decisions

In a world where we're taught to constantly seek external validation, it is essential to learn how to listen to and trust our own thoughts and emotions. Every human has a different vantage point and perspective of their world, made up of both limiting and empowering belief systems developed through their own experiences, traumas, programming, knowledge, and wisdom.

We have much to learn from each other, however, it is important to begin with knowing ourselves as an individual. This is where personal resonance comes in. Personal resonance allows us to tap into our own thoughts, beliefs and feelings by asking ourselves: "What do I believe? Why do I believe that? How do I feel? Is that feeling limiting or empowering?" Developing this kind of self-understanding helps us to make the best choices and decisions as we move through life.

Sometimes when an idea, person or situation comes along you feel resistance to it. This may be because it's new and feels scary so it's expanding and challenging your current circumstances or belief systems. Or you may be sensing that this idea, person or situation is not a good match for you. Having a technique to understand why you do or don't resonate with something will empower you to make good decisions.

Other times we face a decision between two or more choices and we don't know which is the right one for us. We try to analyze the different options but end up feeling pulled in both directions. Our confusion makes it hard to move forward because we don't know how to listen to our inner voice and intuitive knowing.

Everything is energy. We feel and interact with energy all the time. It's not just a New Age woo-woo idea, it's scientific fact. If you've ever walked into a room and feel you could cut the tension with a knife, it's energy you're interacting with. If you've experienced a gut feeling when you walk into your house that something is bothering your loved one before you interact with them, that's energy at work.

It's essential that you learn to understand your own feelings and beliefs so you can distinguish between something that is genuinely not the right choice for you and resistance coming from fear, trauma or limiting beliefs.

This Personal Resonance technique relies on your own personal wisdom by tapping into your feelings and energy. It uses present moment awareness to assess the idea, person or situation that is creating resistance or confusion.

Steps

1. Slow down. Take a few deep breaths. Feel your body without moving. Feel your energy. How are you feeling? How does it feel to take a few deep breaths? Find your center. Feel your feet on the ground. If desired, place your hand on your heart center.

2. While breathing, think about the idea, person or circumstance you are questioning. How does your body feel? Is it tight or anxious? Open, comfortable, or feeling any other sensation? Try to zoom in on where you are feeling sensations. Are they associated with what you are contemplating?

If you are feeling any uncomfortable sensations, ask yourself these questions:

- Is this idea, person or situation coming up against something I previously/currently believe? If so, is that belief limiting or empowering?
- Is this feeling associated with my ideals clashing with others around me?
- Is this feeling associated with fear?
- Is this something I can grow through now?
- If not: Is this something I can work on growing through to prepare for a future similar circumstance?
- If not: Is this something I have no current desire to grow with? Why?

Case study
Susan was shopping for new homes and was struggling to make a choice. She sat down and started to breathe consciously and check in with her feelings. She noticed that she felt overwhelmed and had a tightness and anxious feeling in her chest. Her stomach felt like it was in a knot. Susan adjusted her breathing to be deeper.

She then started to think about the two homes she had to choose from. They both had benefits and downfalls, including one being a larger investment. Instead of using the analyzing part of her brain, she used her imagination to feel what it would be like to live in the first house. She imagined coming home to cook dinner in the kitchen, tucking the kids into bed, entertaining guests, and giving tours of the house. She imagined signing the papers for the house. She took a breath, and checked in with her body. Susan noticed a shift in how she was feeling before she started.

She then thinks about the second house in the same imaginative way and compares how she felt to the first house. She felt less anxious and more at peace thinking about the first house. Susan realized that she felt fearful about how much more the first house cost. She knew that she'd rather spend more for a house that she truly loved than buy a house she didn't. This realization made it much easier to move forward into the physical logistics of buying a house knowing where she stood and why.

Tips for coaches
Remember that this exercise is something that is *practiced*. A client may need lots of practice to begin learning how they are feeling or why. That's *okay*. You can guide them to dig deeper by asking open ended questions that focus on what they think, and why.

While this can be done while interacting with clients, it's also a perfect tool to teach them to practice it on their own.

Personal resonance allows one to learn to trust their own inner voice, truth, and knowing. Learning and using personal resonance helps to allow one to shift over time into their desired life.

RESPONSE ABILITY: ARE YOU IN CHARGE OF YOUR THOUGHTS AND ACTIONS?

By Rebecca Privilege

This exercise helps you understand where you're not taking responsibility in your life. It'll show you how to move from a victim role to feeling empowered and in charge of your own experience. It's for anyone that blames other people for their problems or is stuck feeling unhappy or dissatisfied with their life.

Great for:

- People suffering from anxiety, depression, anger, shame or guilt.
- People who feel like they never catch a break even though they are a good person.
- People ready to take charge of their own lives.

- - -

When clients first come to me wanting to make changes in their life or in their partner's or children's lives, I ask them this question: "Who is responsible for making that change?"

Most will say, "I am". Those that want to change their partner or their children will say "You are" meaning me, or, "They are". If they are wanting to change their partner or children, I keep asking the question until they realize that they are 100% responsible for changing themselves and that they are 100% not responsible for changing others.

Once you have accepted 100% responsibility for making changes in your own life, you can focus your attention on that change and start moving forward.

So what does taking responsibility mean? It's the ability to respond to whatever is happening in your life. When you take 100% ownership for every experience in your life, that doesn't mean everything is your fault. For example, if you've been the victim of a crime or domestic violence or bullying, you are not at fault because you did not commit the offense. However, you are completely responsible for the way you react to that event and how that event affects you and your life, moving forward.

The same applies to other areas of life where there is potential for conflict. For example, if there is trouble in your marriage, you must take responsibility for your role in the relationship. Regardless of what has happened to create the situation, even if it is not your fault, it is still your responsibility. You have the power to rectify the situation, if you choose.

The Cause versus Effect exercise

Do you take control of the direction of your life or are you a victim of circumstance? Where do you operate from: "Cause" or "Effect"?

Let's have a look at this on a piece of paper or on a whiteboard. On the right hand side is the word "Effect". Here is where we believe:
- Things happen *to* me
- I get angry
- I am the victim
- I always look for and have excuses
- I focus on the problem/s, poor me
- I am completely disempowered – I have handed my personal power over to someone or something

Let's look at the left hand side, the "Cause" side. Here is where:
- I am happy
- I am in charge of me and my life
- I'm driving my "bus"
- I am the victor
- I move forward
- I have the ability to respond to any situation
- I am empowered

When you move from Effect into Cause, the solution is easier to find.

So where do you think bullies sit? Yes, in "Effect". Why? Because they hand their power over to whatever negative emotions they are choosing to sit in. For example, bullies are often angry (perhaps at an injustice in their life), sad, hurt with feelings of shame and often guilt for what they are doing. Bullies are choosing to stay a victim of these negative emotions. I say *choosing* because we all have a choice. We can choose to stay in the negative (Effect) or choose to move across to the positive (Cause). When we choose to move from the negative to the positive, we can find solutions.

If your perception is that the person or situation is out of your control, you are choosing to sit in "Effect." If you choose to believe the situation is a positive one and that you can do something to resolve it, then you are sitting in "Cause."

If you are having a discussion with a colleague at work or someone at home, and they do not understand your point of view, you need to take 100% responsibility for the fact that your meaning is not understood. Then you need to take a different approach so that you are communicating effectively. You can't blame them for not understanding you if you are not being clear in your communication. It is always your responsibility, not theirs, to ensure they understand you.

So, it is important to understand that no matter whether the event or person is positive or negative, what matters most is your reaction. Your reaction determines whether you are operating from an empowered (Cause) or disempowered position (Effect).

When you take full ownership of this idea, you have the ability to change and improve any situation. When you accept total responsibility, you are sitting in, and operating at "Cause". Wow, how empowering!

Case Study: Sandra and Kevin (names have been changed to protect their privacy)

Kevin and Sandra and their children (aged 10, 12 and 17) were clients who came to me for help as their family was in complete breakdown mode. All they could do was yell, scream, blame and threaten divorce. In reality, and by their own admission, they had about 4 months until "break" time and were already moving towards separation.

I took all 5 of them individually through the Cause and Effect exercise with an issue specific to them. For Kevin, it was getting angry when the children didn't do their jobs around the house, such as taking the recycling out of the house and into the recycling bin each day.

Kevin very quickly realized that he was sitting in Effect about this relatively minor issue. If the children chose not to do these jobs, then that was their choice. Kevin understood that no amount of yelling, screaming, shouting, or reminding was changing the fact that the children would sometimes not take the recycling out in the morning. He saw that in the overall scheme of things, it didn't matter if the recycling wasn't done daily and to his surprise, the world didn't stop revolving. Once he let go of being a victim of his own "Why is this happening to me" belief, he relaxed and found the children automatically did the jobs they were responsible for doing. Once he stopped getting angry, the children got their power back too and took responsibility for their role in the family.

The Cause and Effect exercise is a great exercise for individuals and families, regardless of age. Tip: with children under 15 (who don't have an eating challenge) I will talk about Cause and Effect in a way that's appropriate to their age. When we talk about the word Cause, I ask them for their absolute favorite food. When we talk about Effect, I ask them for a food they really don't like. So, for example, Cause could be spaghetti bolognaise and Effect is often brussel sprouts (they get such a bad wrap!). I then ask, "Would you like to be eating spaghetti bolognaise or brussel sprouts?" Of course they want to eat the food they like the best, so we talk about how they can stay at Cause and eat spaghetti bolognaise versus being in Effect and eating yucky brussel sprouts. This visual metaphor works a treat and makes it easier for them to understand, and for the family as a whole to talk about.

LISTENING WITH YOUR HEART AND BUILDING A FOUNDATION FOR GENUINE COMMUNICATION

By Leo Castrence

This exercise will help you create a solid foundation to communicate with others in a vulnerable and grounded way. You'll learn how to listen to other people without interrupting and to speak from your heart. It's for anyone who is looking to improve their communication within their personal and business relationships.

Great for:

- Improving communication in personal relationships to avoid yelling, anger and frustration.
- Improving how comfortable people feel communicating honestly and authentically.
- Team-building and bonding in organizations and teams.
- Building trust between coaches and their clients.

The key to having clear communication starts with listening to the person talking. Learning how to listen properly will help you work through communication issues or barriers that leave you feeling unheard or misunderstood.

Many people struggle to genuinely communicate, especially during stressful moments and when they're feeling emotionally triggered. Expressing our emotions and feelings becomes more difficult to navigate if we don't understand how to listen. People who struggle with communication have a tendency to react emotionally or lead the conversation into a debate or argument, rather than respond clearly.

This exercise teaches you how to listen, be present, patient, and compassionate towards both yourself and the other person expressing themselves. You will practice listening and speaking from a deep heart space to improve your communication in your personal and business relationships.

Exercise:

- With your partner (or client) find a comfortable and private space to practice with no distractions.
- Sit across from each other face-to-face, at eye level.
- Have a timekeeper/stopwatch with you (mobile phones have one in the clock application). It's recommended to place your phone out of sight so you don't get distracted.
- If you don't have a person to practice this exercise with, you may use a mirror and look yourself in the eyes.

This exercise begins in complete silence.

Step 1: Eye contact

1. Sit and stare into each other's eyes for 1 minute. No talking, just staring.

Explore and take turns sharing your experience with one another for 3–5 minutes. Was there any resistance you had keeping eye contact with your partner? What emotions came up for you? Did you break eye contact? If so, why? Did you struggle with the silence? How do you feel?

2. Keep eye contact with your partner in silence for 3 minutes.

Explore and take turns sharing your experience with one another for 5–10 minutes. How did this experience feel? How comfortable were you during that experience? What was more challenging, being the listener or speaker? Why so? Take a moment to reflect on where these challenges manifest in your everyday communication.

Step 2: Eye contact with Dialogue

1. Each of you will take 2 minutes speaking on things you are grateful for in your life while the other silently listens. As the listener you will not reply or respond to anything your partner is sharing. Keep your facial expressions at a minimum. Try to avoid nodding in reassurance, and simply keep eye contact. Just listen with your ears and heart, and hold an intention for your partner to feel safe when sharing.

- Explore and share your experience with one another for 3–5 minutes.
- What was more challenging, the listener or speaker? Why so? Take a moment to reflect on where these challenges manifest in your everyday communication. Would keeping eye contact or listening more help de-escalate arguments?

2. Now each of you take 3 minutes to share your deepest fears while the other person listens. If for any moment the speaker runs out of things to share or hits a mental or emotional block, the listener may prompt with the question "What is your deepest fear?" As the listener you hold the space for your partner to explore what they want to share.

- Explore and share your experience with one another for 5–10 minutes.
- How difficult was it for you to be vulnerable with someone willing to listen? How do you feel after expressing yourself in a vulnerable way?

Step 3: Eye contact in silence

Finally, you will sit again in silence, staring into each other's eyes for 5 minutes. Take these 5 minutes to be present in gratitude for yourself and your partner for their presence and vulnerability.

- Explore and share your experience with one another for 5–10 minutes.
- How did the silence feel? What thoughts or feelings came up? How present did you feel? How can you take this experience with you to future conversations?

Questions used during this exercise can be changed to whatever question resonates with the situation or client.

Listening during challenging communications provides us with the opportunity to check our own emotions and triggers. It prevents us from a reactive and emotional rebuttal that can easily turn into arguments or even screaming matches. Listening first before speaking also sets an example about how you expect to be treated when you're speaking. Explore what it felt like to be the listener and not have the ability to speak. Can you envision yourself having the same presence when talking and listening to others?

For more resources visit here:https://actualizedaffinity.com/building-a-foundation-for-genuine-communication/

TAP INTO YOUR INTERNAL GUIDANCE SYSTEM FOR DECISION MAKING

By Claire Costello

This exercise gives you a stress-freeing tool that can become a daily fun practice of establishing a relationship with your true self. Use it to find your internal compass so you can make decisions with ease. It's for anyone who is struggling with making big (and everyday) decisions and wants to create and live their ideal reality.

Great for:

- People who struggle to make decisions or are anxious they might make the "wrong" choice.
- People who live too much in their head and want to tap into their intuitive side.
- Entrepreneurs confused about which opportunities to take. E.g. "It sounds like an amazing opportunity, but it doesn't feel right".

— — —

We all have an Internal Guidance System that we can choose to tap into, listen, trust and follow with profound results. This can also be described as our intuition, instinct, gut response, true self, or soul.

There can be so much going on in life, business and relationships that making choices can get overwhelming and stressful. You may try to make decisions only from your logical mind or from fear, which can result in feelings of stuckness, struggle and regret that you made the "wrong" choice.

When we learn how to recognize the unique language that is guiding us from within, we can choose to live so much more at peace, feel greater fulfillment and be more clear and confident about our direction in business, relationships, health and life!

113

Some benefits of tapping into our Inner Wisdom are:

- Clarity of path, purpose and more passionate living,
- Self-confidence, self-love and trust of self,
- Living in an effortless flow state,
- Ability to come back to personal center,
- Health, energy and vitality in the physical body,
- More peace, joy and stability,
- Authentic *Being* and living,
- Empowered to take action to move towards goals,
- Courage to try new things, take leaps of faith and live outside the "box",
- Having amazing opportunities and synchronicities come our way.

Step 1: Get into a clear and centered space
Choose one or more of the following methods that best supports you to be in a clear space within yourself. Feeling relaxed, peaceful in the mind and present in the body massively supports clear decision-making.

Do this before moving onto Step 2. (This can be different or the same each time).

Ways of doing this:

- Movement – walking, running, shaking, swimming, yoga, dancing.
- Breathing – breathwork, intentional breathing.
- Journaling – gratitude, expressing feelings, emotions and thoughts.
- Releasing – shaking/tapping/expressing/stating intentions to let go. Release trapped emotions, thoughts, other people's influences, judgments, opinions and any doubts, fears, limitations or resistances you may be holding onto.
- Connect to your center with intention – call in clarity of your destined path, truth and alignment.
- Tune in to your core values– bring your focus and attention within for self-reflection – What are my *authentic* desires? Needs? Expressions? Intentions at this time?

- Gratitude.
- Meditation – be fully present in the moment, body, breath, sensations.

During your chosen activity/s, allow what wants to arise to show itself and then write down any feelings or insights you get.

The following 2 steps are key to recognizing your Inner Guidance System by establishing your personal signals of what a Yes and No is. These signs will show up in your body as sensations, words or images.

Step 2: Establishing what your *full body* Yes is

Once in a clear space, say to your true self, "Show me a *clear Yes*". Notice what arises and note the answers to these questions:

- What am I experiencing in my body? E.g. a lightness, heart opening, peace, comfort, excitement, joy, an ability to breathe fully, expansion, goosebumps.
- Do I see anything visually? e.g. a color, a symbol, an open door.
- Notice if/how the body wants to move and the direction–hand opens, a foot moves forwards, your head shifts, a pulsation, a flinch, etc.
- How does my belly feel?
- Women – How does my womb feel?
- Do any words want to be spoken – e.g. YES, ahhhh, mmmm or a Yay!

Step 3: Establish what your No is

It is very important to identify your clear NO or non-confirmation for this choice. You can ask yourself, "Show me a *clear No* – i.e. this is not the best decision for me (at this time)". Ask yourself these questions:

- How does this feel? E.g. heavy, dull, contracted, shaky, painful, nauseous, a strong gut response, blocked, (Women - signals from your womb wisdom).
- What is the emotion? E.g. sad, angry, frustrated, resistance.
- Is there a vision? There may be a different color, symbol, a closed door.
- How does your body/posture want to move this time?
- Any words or sounds that were to be expressed? E.g. Ugh, Agh, NO.

Step 4: What are your choices?

Think about the decision you need to make and write down the different choices you have. Be clear and specific. Write, draw or use objects to symbolize your different options.

Often it is worth including "Other" because there may be another possibility that you haven't thought of yet. "Other" would include "no clear answer yet", it may be necessary for an unfolding of circumstances that goes beyond the limitations of your current thinking, conditioning and beliefs.

Step 5: Tune into each choice

Tune into each of your different options, one a time. Do this either through writing and/or you can change places/cushions where you are sitting or standing so you can feel a clear difference between the options.

Go back to your full body Yes in between the options for comparison. Notice the difference in your body, posture, breath, movement, level of comfort. Note down your experience at each step.

You can repeat if you feel you need more clarity.

Step 6: Make this a joyful daily practice for any decision

Practice this exercise for any kind of decisions, big or small. E.g. Does my body want to eat this or this? Will it be most beneficial to be at this event tonight?

You will be amazed by the results. Connection with intuition improves, decision-making is quicker and life gets easier, healthier (and more magical!) through practice.

Tips for coaches
This exercise is very supportive when someone can hold space through the process. A coach can guide a client through these steps, empower the client (without imposing opinion/influence) by asking the above open questions for the client to find their own internal wisdom, e.g. How does this feel? What do you notice in your body? Do you sense a difference?

Having the client share their process helps them to identify and get clear on what they really want, what is/has been blocking and how to move forwards. Working deeper with the client (e.g. inner child, shadow work, trauma release) to see and release any blockages is often required in Step 1 before one is able to receive a full body Yes.

WHAT'S YOUR VALUE? MOVING FROM AWARENESS TO POSSIBILITY IN RELATIONSHIPS

By Selena Ardelean

This exercise will help you discover your personal values and empower you to better understand the dynamics of the relationships in which you struggle. It's for anyone that is considering making a big change in their lives or is having difficulties in their personal or professional relationships. You can also use this exercise in business settings and in organizations where people need to be "on the same page".

Great for:

- People considering big changes like switching jobs or changing careers.
- People going through a culture shock (changing countries, facing divorce or a break-up).
- Managers/team leaders leading a new or merged team.

— — —

One of the most interesting challenges in communication is understanding exactly what your partner in conversation is talking about. How much we are able to grasp the other person's message is heavily influenced by how we see the world. We generally look at people, situations and events through the filter of our own points of reference. We're often not even aware that we're doing this because these points of reference exist in our subconscious mind.

When things are going wrong in a work or personal relationship, it's necessary to have a clear view of what each person's values are in order to be able to understand possible communication challenges and overcome unnecessary stress. Once you can see the other person's perspective, then you are better equipped to resolve the conflict or move forward in a positive way.

118

Elena, 44 years old, mom of 2 young children had been facing a difficult time for a year before she came to see me. She had a 9-5 job as an administrative employee and a husband who was travelling a lot. Caught between her work, family and personal needs, she was facing burnout and divorce. This exercise allowed her to understand that she and her husband did not share the same values: while her core values were "family" and "security", her husband was living his life from the values of "adventure" and "efficiency". Once Elena saw the difference in the points of view, she was able to have an open discussion with her husband about what their individual needs were and decided to revise their contributions to the relationship.

If you are a business coach, corporate coach, a parent, or in a relationship, this exercise will help you discover your personal values and empower you to better understand the dynamics of the relationships in which you struggle.

You will need:

- A values list (you can find online)
- A separate sheet of paper
- Colored pens (at least 3 colors)
- A timer

Getting prepared
Decide on what aspect of your personal/professional life you are going to apply the exercise to. Print a list of values (you can find these easily online) and have it at hand.
Examples of values include:

- adventure
- comfort
- connection
- efficiency
- family
- freedom
- kindness

- integrity
- intelligence
- security
- success
- wisdom
- wealth

The goal of the exercise is: to determine what your core values are and help you become aware of your way of perceiving reality through the filter of your values. There are no right/ wrong answers.

Take a few deep breaths before starting.

Identifying your core values

1. Intuitively choose those values that you most resonate with and circle them with one of the colored pens. Allow 5 seconds per word, and not longer than 10 minutes for the entire list. You might resonate with all the values in the list but only circle the ones that you feel are *really important* to you. If you don't understand one word or are stuck over-thinking it, just keep moving on to the next words on the list.
2. Go over the circled values and select 20 out of the entire list, intuitively. Circle the new choices with a different colored pen. Allow 3 minutes maximum to do this.
3. Select 10 of the 20 values you've selected and circle them with a different color. Allow 1 minute for this.
4. Write the 10 values on the separate piece of paper.
5. Circle 5 out of the 10 remaining values and rank them in order of their importance from 1-5 where 1 is the most important value.
6. Rewrite your top 2 values. These are your core values and are basically giving you an indication of your needs that must be fulfilled at present. These 2 values will decide on the priorities you set for yourself and how you make decisions.

Understanding your values

Take a moment and answer the following questions:
- How do you feel about your values?
- Why do you think these values are important to you?
- How do you live your values on a daily basis? List examples of living your values.

Your values and personal patterns

Brainstorm and identify your personal patterns in:

a. A situation or context when your values were respected, and
b. A situation or context when your values were dismissed
   What did you feel? What did you think? What did you do?

Finishing

Close by congratulating yourself for your bravery. Acknowledge your effort of being willing to go deep into your subconscious mind and embrace new insights.

End with an exploration mission: Pick one of the values on your top 10 list and live it in all the ways possible, recognize it in different contexts and express it whenever you need or want to.

Tips for coaches:

- When observing the exercise, pay attention to the stress elements surfacing during the exercise and discuss them using the final list of values for those who felt stress. Be creative and intuitive as well.
- Be strict on the timing. Most of the times the client wants to do "things right" and feel the need to really make sure they have "the best" answer.
- Allow enough time for the debriefing. Experience has taught me that keeping the room silent for 5 minutes after having completed the exercise brings up gems in terms of personal awareness, aha moments and realizations.

Whenever possible, repeat the exercise after 6 months in order to record or track any change in the list, as well as in the client's needs and priorities.

Career Compass: Identify Your Interests, Skills and Values to Choose the Right Career Path for You

By Erika Fitzgibbon

This exercise helps you identify your best career path based on your personal interests and skills, free from the external influences of family and society. It's for people that feel stuck or confused about their career, people with multiple career interests or those feeling pressured to follow in the footsteps of their family.

Great for:

- People with multiple interests and skills trying to decide on a career path.
- People that feel pressured to pursue a career they don't love.
- People that don't have a clear idea of what career they would enjoy.
- People wanting to pivot careers, get back into the workforce or start their own business.

– – –

Making career choices throughout your life can be challenging, especially if we have multiple interests and skills or feel pressured to continue with a career that we don't love.

This exercise is designed to raise your awareness of your own skills and interests, expand the realm of possible careers you might enjoy, and help empower you to "go your own way" instead of feeling pushed into a career that doesn't feel right.

This exercise is based on the work of John Holland and Dr. Murray Bowen, two respected professionals from the worlds of career psychology and family systems theory. In the first part you will identify your personality types and areas of interest. In the second you will review the familial and societal factors that may have influenced your career decisions.

This exercise will be especially helpful if you're considering career options where your interests, skills and values aren't aligned with the popular choice of your family or society.

Step 1: Identify your top 3 personal Holland themes
Read each of the six theme descriptions below and write the names of the three themes that describe you 1. the best, 2. second best and, 3. third best.

First, think of the things you enjoyed most in your childhood, adolescence and adulthood: toys, games, activities, hobbies, interests, classes, risks taken, or topics researched. Next, underline the words that stand out most to you and resonate with you as important across your life-span. Even if you aren't great at these skills now, if they are an important part of your identity, be sure to include them.

Realistic – People who have athletic or mechanical ability, prefer to work with objects, machines, tools, plants, or animals, or to be outdoors.
Interests: Machines, computer networks, athletics, working outdoors
Activities: Operating equipment, using tools, building, repairing, providing security
Skills: Mechanical ingenuity and dexterity, physical coordination
Values: Tradition, practicality, common sense

Investigative – People who like to observe, learn, investigate, analyze, evaluate, or solve problems.
Interests: Science, medicine, math, research
Activities: Performing lab work, solving problems, conducting research
Skills: Mathematical ability, researching, writing, analyzing
Values: Independence, curiosity, learning

Artistic – People who have artistic, innovating or intuitional abilities, and like to work in unstructured situations, using their imagination or creativity.
Interests: Self-expression, art appreciation, communication, culture

Activities: Composing music, performing, writing, creating visual art
Skills: Creativity, musical ability, artistic expression
Values: Beauty, originality, independence, imagination

Social – People who like to work with people – to inform, enlighten, help, train, develop, or cure them, or are skilled with words.
Interests: People, teamwork, healing, community service
Activities: Teaching, caring for people, counseling, training employees
Skills: People skills, verbal ability, listening, showing understanding
Values: Cooperation, generosity, service to others

Enterprising – People who like to work with people – influencing, persuading, leading or managing for organizational goals or for economic gain.
Interests: Business, politics, leadership, entrepreneurship
Activities: Selling, managing, persuading, marketing
Skills: Verbal ability, ability to motivate & direct others
Values: Risk taking, status, competition, influences

Conventional – People who like to work with data, have clerical or numerical ability, carrying things out in detail or following through on others instructions.
Interests: Organization, data management, accounting, investing, information systems
Activities: Setting up systems, organizing, keeping records, developing computer apps
Skills: Ability to work with numbers, data analysis, finances, attention to detail
Values: Accuracy, stability, efficiency

(Based on John Holland's vocational personalities from *Making Vocational Choices: A Theory of Careers*, 3rd Edition, Psychological Assessments Resources, 1997.)

Step 2: List your most influential family members

We are all influenced by a strong pull that exists within our families. Bowen Family Systems is a theory of human behavior that views the family as an emotional unit where its members are intensely connected. We solicit each other's attention, approval and support, and react to each other's needs, expectations and upsets. The connectedness and emotional reactivity make the functioning of family members interdependent. Families differ somewhat in their degree of interdependence but it is always present to some degree.

List the important people in your family. Write down your closest family members while in childhood, adolescence and adulthood. Include parents, guardians, step parents, grandparents, siblings, aunts, uncles and cousins. You might also include close family friends, neighbors, important teachers and mentors as well. Also include people with careers you admire.

Step 3: Identify themes for your influential family members

For each person you have listed write down their career, hobbies, and interests. What were their accomplishments? Which Holland personality types and values are most closely related to each member of your family and those with careers you admire.

Step 4: Look for important patterns in your answers

Think about the values in your family, the work you currently do, the society in which you were raised and that in which you now live.

- Are your interests similar/dissimilar to your family, work or society?
- Who in your family had the most influence on you?
- Did your family members often talk about their careers or work? Was the talk positive/negative?
- What messages did you get about careers and work while you were growing up?
- Does your current work reflect your number one interest theme?

Step 5: Deciding on your next career steps
How can you use this new awareness to formulate your next career steps? What can you start doing? Stop doing? What are the obstacles? Do you need to build support for your interests? Can you increase your happiness by integrating these interests and values in your hobbies?

Case study
Suzie has been trying to figure out what to do with her career after she has spent some time out of the workforce raising her two daughters. She is considering going back to graduate school, re-opening her photography business or perhaps pursuing a new third option that doesn't seem clear.

Suzie identifies herself as: Social, Artistic, and Enterprising (Holland Themes). This is how she categories her most influential family members, the people she admires and her society:

Mom: Realistic & Social - Surgical nurse, many friends, collector of art.
Dad: Enterprising, Artistic & Realistic - Worked in sales/printing, liked music/camping.
Brothers: - Realistic, Enterprising - Outdoorsy, business owners.
Grandparents: - Realistic & Artistic - Built own home, bicycling/painting hobbies.
Admires: Social - change makers, women who fight for equal rights.
Society: Enterprising - Strong messages about making money and status in the media.

Suzie sees her personal path has always been more in the Social and Artistic categories and realizes she's been strongly influenced by her mostly Realistic family. From her discoveries with this exercise Suzie decides her best choice is to develop a business combining mental health coaching and photography, while donating a portion of her revenues to local non-profit organizations to help women.

FEEL THE PULL OF NATURE AND CONNECT TO YOUR INNER TRUTH

By Daniel Brisbon

This exercise empowers you to connect with your own inner truth by listening and feeling into your intuitive side out in nature. It's for people that have a strong connection with nature, desire a deeper connection within themselves or need to make an important decision. You can also use this exercise with clients if you have access to nature or any outdoor space.

Great for:

- Outdoor enthusiasts that want to connect with their intuition
- People that desire a greater attunement to their own inner-wisdom
- People that are stuck in life with a situation or challenge that requires a decision
- Transformational coaches with good access to nature

In today's world it can be easy to become overwhelmed by the constant movement and change in the outside world. TV, computer and phone screens take up a good chunk of your time and attention and with all this connection to the outside world it can be easy to slowly lose connection within yourself. This is why time spent in nature can help you disconnect from technology and reconnect to you.

Listening to where your intuition is guiding you to go while you're in the wilderness, rather than where your logical mind thinks you should go, can bring great revelations into understanding your goals and needs on a deeper level. Being in nature gets you out of your head and into your heart. Nature is an amazing place to connect with your intuition and ask for answers to the problems or challenges you face.

From where you ultimately feel pulled to sit in nature, you are given the gift of seeing and understanding what answers nature might have for you. The lucid stream you come upon can show you that you need to learn to flow and be adaptable within your own life. The trees swaying in the wind can show you that strong roots are much more important than how you look. That mountain in the distance may show you that challenges in life are needed for us to grow and rather than dwelling on the struggle, you need to shift your perception to understanding that the journey to the top may be tough, but the views are worth the pain.

Rather than focusing on the external struggles that your mind is constantly trying to solve, this exercise trains you to explore what is beneath the surface. What is lying in waiting within your unconscious mind that can be brought to the surface? You can go around in circles tackling the issues you are facing in the outside world (career, relationships, finances), but in the stillness of the wilderness you are able to tap into what your intuition and higher self is trying to communicate. The answers you need are already inside of you.

Steps

1. Be quiet and practice listening internally and feeling the "pull" into nature. Visualize with your mind's eye showing you where you need to go and not what your physical eyes are telling you.
2. Be patient and remember to breathe slowly as you listen within yourself. This isn't a race, but rather a chance to be connected with yourself and the land. It's more important to move slowly and methodically than rushing through the process.
3. Use the senses. Feel what they are telling you. Trust your intuition and trust your gut on what direction you need to go. Learn to let go of the past and future and practice being fully present in the moment as you are guided from within yourself.

4. From this same place of feeling, feel where your inner pull is taking you. It could be a short hike to your destination or it could be a few feet away from where you are standing.

5. As you move out on the land, staying connected to the present moment, ask yourself these questions: What am I noticing? What is this telling/teaching me? What am I learning more about myself as I listen to my own inner wisdom?

Tips
Be patient. This exercise requires some time and patience because the volume on the dial between your physical mind and your intuition may not be turned up that high to start out. The point is to tap into your intuition and gut instinct so it may take a while, but it is worth it!

Be quiet and trust the process. Practicing this exercise in silence is crucial. Feel the earth beneath your shoes, or better yet, go barefoot. Smell the fresh air and feel the direction of the breeze on your face. Listen to sounds of the wilderness while also listening to the sounds of your own inner wilderness. Let go of what the eyes are seeing and the mind is thinking and concentrate on what the heart is saying and where your intuition is guiding you.

Case study
Several years ago I had the privilege of implementing this exercise with a close friend of mine. As we hiked through the forest, with the leaves and pine needles crunching underneath our shoes, we finally came to the spot that my friend felt pulled to sit as she started to share with me about her own personal struggles.

Expectations from friends and family in her personal life were taking a toll on her and she was battling some physical sickness on top of that. And instead of being hung up on the people putting high expectations on her and her physical ailments, we decided to listen and dive deeper.

As the trees blew violently from the strong winds above us, she was able to come to a profound realization. The strongest trees around weren't the most rigid trees that were unaffected by the wind, but rather the trees that were able to move and sway and dance with the wind. She then quickly understood that she needs to do the same in her personal life. Rather than put up walls and try to be strong she needed to learn to roll with the punches and that her inner strength could handle the strong winds.

That is the power of this exercise when done correctly. It can train us to learn to listen to ourselves on a deeper level than we can ever imagine. All we need is to be patient and open. And some beautiful open space never hurts too.

Tips for coaches
This exercise is perfect to use with clients that have a strong connection with nature and are desiring a deeper connection within themselves. Use it for the beginning of a coaching session to set the tone for the rest of the session.

Invite your client to attune to their senses (smell, sound, taste) as they move through nature. Encourage your clients to listen and feel rather than think and see with their eyes. This exercise is fun and can be a little adventurous, but be sure to always stay safe and in safe places in nature with your client.

WHAT'S YOUR WELL-BEING NUMBER?

By Tim Dean

This exercise helps you consciously evaluate all areas of your life so you can identify which life area will bring you the biggest improvement in well-being. It's for anyone that wants a simple way to identify their professional and/or personal goals so they know where to focus their efforts.

Great for:

- People to decide what's important for them to prioritize in their life right now.
- People to use before doing a goal-setting exercise.
- Coaches to use in their first session with new clients to decide on a priority area to focus on for improvement.

- - -

Whether you're getting ready to work with a coach or you're gearing up to make changes in your life, it's critical to know what your priorities are and what you need to work on.

In my coaching practice, when I start working with an individual I ask them, "What do you want?" It's common for this question to be followed by a lengthy silence. Or a person may state many variations of what they *don't want*, i.e., "I don't want to be a parent that isn't around for my kids," or "I don't want to be the type of boss that isn't respected." It's a lot easier for someone to share what they don't want versus what they do want.

A simple and effective solution to transform your "nots" into "wants" is to use this *What's Your Well-Being Number?* exercise. Once you identify your true wants, you not only become more receptive to a possible coaching partnership, you also discover your most urgent priorities of what you are looking to achieve or advance in your own life.

Use these 2 steps to help you consciously acknowledge what you want for yourself:

1. The Scenario

Think about all the professional and personal aspects of your life: from career aspirations and family dynamics to financial goals, current health, key relationships, lifestyle, etc.

Close your eyes and then mentally "collect" all of these life aspects into one large imaginary box. Think of your current career, your relationships, your health, your lifestyle, etc., all collected together in one space.

Then ask yourself, using a scale of 1 to 10 (1=all of my areas are in complete disarray; 10=all areas are exactly where I want them to be), "What number am I today?" It is completely OK if your answer is a single digit or a range (e.g. 6-7). Now move on to Step 2.

2. The Follow-up question

Now ask yourself, "What would make my number higher?"

This follow-up question is the more important and relevant one, as it allows you to contemplate, maybe for the first time in a while, which life area is the top priority for you right now. Consciously acknowledging this information provides key insights into what part of your life you want to address and/or improve first.

For example, if your life right now overall feels like a 7, ask yourself, "What would make my life feel more like an 8 or 9?" The life area that comes to mind first indicates which area you should be focusing on to achieve a more fulfilling life. For example, you realize that your health is stopping you from achieving a lot of your important goals. Or you feel that working on your relationships would improve bring your well-being number up to an 8 or 9.

Tip: Avoid averages

After Step 1, you may want to assign each area its own "number" from 1 to 10, and then take the average to determine your overall well-being number. For example, while your health feels ideal (say, 8 or 9), you feel your career is less than optimal (a 3 or 4). So you think, "I'm a 6."

This exercise is not about averaging individual numbers for each life area. It is consciously gathering all areas of your life into one space, and then evaluating where you feel holistically, right now, on a 1-10 scale. The reason for this is because you're not picking the part of your life that has the lowest rating, you're identifying what you can work on that will have the biggest impact on your well-being right now.

It's a good idea to repeat this process after you've been working on an area of your life so you can reevaluate what your new priority for improvement is.

UNPACKING YOUR IDENTITY AND CHALLENGING YOUR LABELS

By Kerry LiBrando

This exercise helps you examine different components of your identity to inspire a new awareness of the labels you wear personally, and the labels you prescribe to others. It's for anyone that struggles with their personal identity or self-worth, and for those that wish for a world with less prejudice and stereotyping.

Great for...

- People looking for a safe way to begin to strip away the "masks" they wear and increase their vulnerability.
- People seeking a deeper understanding and appreciation of their personal identity.
- People wanting to let go of their prejudices and create a more equitable world.

"To let ourselves be seen, deeply seen, vulnerably seen... we're kinder and gentler to the people around us and we're kinder and gentler to ourselves."
Brene Brown, *The Power of Vulnerability*, TEDxHouston, 2010

How many of us shy away from our reflection? How many of us can truly say not only do we SEE our flaws, but we accept them? How often do we see someone in our office, on our walk, while we wait in line at the bank and think, "Hmm, look at that person, they must be _____, because look at _____." And in an instant, WE have decided WHO or WHAT that person is.

Massive research has been published to support the idea that we often project our own fears and flaws onto others. The drive to label, to put others and ourselves into neat, organized and easily seen categories is not a new desire. Our brains are wired for a fear of the unknown in order to protect us from danger. Many people harness this fear to breed curiosity, while others use it to breed hate. How can we SEE ourselves so that we may SEE others? And once we begin to really SEE others, how can our language follow suit to tear down the fear and embrace the unknown?

This exercise allows you to spend time examining your reflection in the mirror to discover what features and flaws you notice. What stories does your face tell? Does your eye color come from your father and point to a certain ethnicity? Does the jewelry you wear in your ears, nose, mouth, etc. point to the culture you were raised in?

Once you have taken time to examine your reflection and what labels reflect the components of your identity, you will find your curiosity deepen. Your awareness will pull at you each time you seek a neat and easy label for another person. Your awareness will challenge you and ask: "Who am I to say WHO that person is?"

Steps

The materials you will need for this exercise:

- A pen/pencil
- Paper
- A mirror
- A timer (either stopwatch or phone would be fine)

1. Find a comfortable and quiet space that you feel would support you in being reflective for anywhere from ten to thirty minutes.

2. Have your mirror and timer handy. Once you are comfortably seated, you will set your timer for 30 seconds. In silence, you will closely examine your facial reflection in the mirror. This feels awkward or uncomfortable for many people. Honor yourself and stick with the silence.

When I have lead this exercise with adolescents, I have verbally suggested beforehand a course for their eyes to travel: from the hairline and the ridges on the forehead and letting their eyes scan from side to side taking in details. This gave them focus and supported their stillness and silence. If you are afraid you may break your silence, try this!

3. For 30 seconds, you should just notice. This is not the space or time to judge, approve, shame, or push away. Send your face compassion and strength. What do you see in the details of your face?

4. When the timer goes off, spend a minute or two and write down your observations.

My personal observations from this exercise:

- My right eyebrow is always raised, now matter my expression
- My forehead has three deep set lines
- My eyes are two different shapes
- One of my eyes looks somewhat droopy
- All of my features are dark: eyes, hair
- My skin is VERY light except my freckles
- My nose is soft and round
- I have a soft chin
- My chin has a scar from falling off my bike
- My ears stick out and are weighed down with earrings
- I have tiny wrinkles at the corners of my mouth

5. Spend some time considering your personal identity and the labels you wear to reflect it. The following categories represent different components of individual identity.

- Race
- National origin
- Ethnicity
- Gender
- First language
- Religious affiliation
- Socio-economic group
- Age
- Ability (physical, emotional, developmental)

136

Read through the list and consider the following questions:

- How do I see myself in that category?
- Where on my face can I see that component of my identity?
- What labels have others given me in this category that I am resisting?

Some of my personal reflections from doing this exercise:

- I racially identify as white and my skin tone certainly reflects that.
- My socio-economic group is upper middle class and I reflect that in the money I do investing in keeping my hair done and highlighted, my eyebrows waxed, and my diamond earrings in my ears.
- My gender is female and I think I reflect it in the softness of my face.
- My dark features point to my Irish heritage. This is where I have often been prescribed a label of "drunk" and "lazy" that historically has been associated with Irish culture.

6. Reflect for a moment and think back to an instance where you labeled another person without inviting conversation or curiosity. Where have I given a label to another person's identity?

This work is often uncomfortable and may make you feel shame for thoughts and actions in the past. It is ok to own and admit that you once spoke, act, and thought from a place of less knowledge. But, now that you know better, you can begin to DO better. Acknowledging where we have room to grow and do better is difficult, but necessary for us to make our lives and our communities more supportive and equitable.

PART 4: GOALS AND HABITS

Goal-setting –Motivation - Daily practices

ANNUAL GOAL SETTING WORKSHOP

By Samuel Hatton

The Annual Goal Setting Workshop helps you live with intention and legacy. It guides you to recognize what is important in your life by identifying goals and themes that you wish to prioritize. It's for anyone who wants to live a purposeful and meaningful life, including couples that want to work toward a common destination.

Great for:

- People who want legacy, meaning and purpose in their life
- People who are trying to draw closer to a significant other
- People who have trouble recognizing opportunities or focusing on the things that are important to them
- Anyone who is working on setting boundaries or has trouble saying "No" to things that keep them busy.

– – –

Each year, from mid-December through mid-January, something incredible happens. Contagious energy sweeps through the collective consciousness and invites each person to assess their year and look forward to the next with optimism. You don't have to do a thing to have access to this energy. It is everywhere. Sometimes we listen to it and make a New Year's Day resolution, other times we ignore it and let doubt get the best of us. Unfortunately, most people let the energy pass them by entirely.

Rather than do nothing, draw upon the new year momentum and maximize it. The Annual Goal Setting Workshop is a simple, yet powerful, process. It will solidify your legacy and create more purpose in your life.

This exercise accelerates individuals toward a life lived well, with meaning, intention, and clarity. Decisions become easier with the help of your goals and especially your annual theme, which provides a basis for distinguishing opportunities from distractions. With this solid framework for getting in the right headspace, brainstorming goals, and selecting goals that fit, effective goal-setting goes from mysterious to easy.

Step 1: Celebrate the previous year's achievements
The purpose of this step is two-fold. First, it's good for legacy, as this becomes part of your personal history. Second, it puts you in a positive mindset of gratitude. This helps set a healthy foundation for positive goal planning.

Go crazy with this one. Write down as many things that you can possibly think of. More is always better when it comes to celebrations and gratitude.

Celebrations may include:

- New traditions
- Travel & trips
- New people in your life
- First-time milestones
- Previous year's accomplishments

Step 2: Summarize your previous year in one word
This helps you put a title on the previous year's chapter and prepares you for crafting your next chapter, the upcoming year.

Make it personal. This becomes a staple in your legacy. It's a way to reflect back on an entire year, and say "YES! This one thing is what my year was about!"

Keep it positive. If all you can think of is a tragedy, try to find the silver lining in it.

Examples:

- Calling - when I heard my destiny calling me
- Fatherhood - when I became a father
- Adventure - the year I lived abroad

Step 3: Determine the theme for next year

What is this next year going to be about? Is it going to be about growth? Is it going to be about living with adventure? Is it going to be about working smarter? Figure out what this next year is going to mean for you. This will help you orient your goals and prioritize them.

Here are some of my own past themes:

- Royal Identity – embracing an attitude of abundance rather than scarcity
- Modeling – studying people with qualities, attitudes, and abilities that I want to have
- Bold Action – focusing on courage and bravery in my daily choices

Step 4: Set goals for the next year

How do you achieve your dreams? You can start by setting goals. Get excited and write your desires. Stretch and write things that seem just out of reach.

To maintain balance in your life set at least a couple goals in various categories. This is good for two reasons: it helps to maintain balance, and it helps to brainstorm goals within areas that you can grow.

Sample categories: Business/Career, Financial, Physical, Mindset/Education, Family, Spiritual, Lifestyle, Relationships.

Choose categories that work for you. I had one client that hated the words "Business" and "Lifestyle", so those categories for him became "Contribution" and "Recreation". Other categories I've seen in other people's models include Travel, Environment, Mastery, Giving.

Two important guidelines for setting goals:

143

(1) Always start a goal with a VERB. This guarantees that your goal is action focused. It's not what you want...it's about what you do.

Examples:

- START an online business
- WRITE an ebook
- SELL 10% more product volume

(2) Make sure to make it S.M.A.R.T

- Specific – Anyone can understand the goal.
- Measurable – You know when it's accomplished.
- Attainable – You can do it. You are in control of the outcome.
- Relevant – It fits into your theme. It fits into who you are.
- Time-bound – It has a timeframe or due date.

Step 5: Choose your top priorities
Priorities help you understand what matters. Not all goals are equal. Some will greatly impact you, or the area of life you've categorized it in. You know what is most important, so trust yourself and choose.

Put a star next to each most important goal in each category. These are your top priorities. Then identify your top 3 overall goals with two stars. Finally, put a third star next to your most important goal.

Write a new list with your top goals, starting with the most important to the least important. This is called "force-ranking".

Feeling stuck? One way to identify your top priority is to ask, "What goal, if accomplished, will make many of my other goals easier or unnecessary?"

Step 6: Identify behaviors to put your goals on auto-pilot
This is where dreams become reality. It's putting legs to your goals. Ask yourself, "What behaviors do you need to create in your life to guarantee that I will accomplish my top priority goal?" You can substitute the word "behaviors" for "action items" or "next steps".

Your behaviors could be daily behaviors (habits), weekly behaviors, monthly behaviors, or one-time behaviors.

For example, you may have a goal to "launch a side business"

- One-time behavior: write a business plan
- Daily behavior: block out 45 minutes daily to work on your side business
- Weekly behavior: meet with an accountability partner or coach

Tips for coaches
- Coaches can choose to take this whole exercise and facilitate it with a client over a 2-hour session or group workshop or they can have the client prep steps 1-5 and do step 6 as a follow-up session. Step 6 can be difficult to do on their own since habit formation doesn't come naturally to most.
- Encourage them to get into a good physiological state (rested and fed).
- If they have a significant other in their life and their goal is oneness, this exercise is very powerful to do with a spouse or life partner.
- Encourage your clients to block out an entire morning, afternoon, or evening. Though this can be done in 1 hour, it's better to take time with it. One effective way to do this is to invite them with a calendar invite of 2 hours and then get them to commit to limiting their distractions during that time. Text them before a word of encouragement. And text them 1 hour after asking them how it went.

For more resources about the exercise in this chapter, visit: https://www.samuelhatton.com/activate-your-life-goal-resources/

PROSPERITY CONSCIOUSNESS: SHIFT YOUR MONEY BLOCKS AND UPGRADE YOUR MONEY MINDSET

By Aoife Gaffney

This exercise will help you remove your unconscious money blocks and map out a path to shift your focus from a scarcity mindset to an abundance mindset. It will help you start living the abundant life you deserve and desire. This exercise is great for anyone who feels stuck in a money rut or feels they are not earning their true worth.

Great for:

- People who want to create more abundance in their life.
- People who are stuck in a scarcity mindset and don't feel good about their financial situation.
- People who have money blocks that are preventing them from having the money they deserve.

– – –

The starting point of all riches is the development of a prosperity consciousness. If you want to be truly wealthy in life, you must first achieve it in your mind.

Both poverty and wealth are the result of a state of mind. The most important single step you will ever take on the road to wealth and financial independence is the decision to change your thinking – to rewire your mind with an unshakable belief that you can and will achieve your money goals. If you get this step right, anything is possible.

The problem is that many people have money blocks. A money block is "anything that holds you back from making the money you want." This is usually an underlying belief or fear surrounding money. You may or may not be aware of it, but it's there. It might sound ridiculous – why would anyone be unconsciously preventing themselves from making more money? But that's what a block is; an unconscious limiting belief that prevents you from achieving what you want.

This exercise will help you remove your unconscious money blocks. It'll help you identify where you currently are, how you value yourself and what areas you need to bring immediate attention to. It will help you start living the abundant life you deserve and desire.

This technique will shift your focus to prosperity and feelings of high self-worth. It will make changes at a cellular level that will allow more abundance to simply flow into your life. Energy flows where focus goes.

What you will need:

1. The nicest notebook or journal you can find.
2. A beautiful pen that you absolutely love.
3. 30 minutes or so of uninterrupted time.

Steps

Use these 5 steps to help shift your focus from a scarcity mindset to an abundance mindset.

1. Use the headings below as a guide to figure out where you currently are in your life, according to your own standards.

Economy	Average	Luxury
Cheapest on the market	It does the job	Even a lottery win would not encourage a change
Embarrassed to show anyone	Not the best but not the worst either	A symbol of wealth, abundance, and achievement
Feels cheap	Functions without being annoying	Reflects your ultimate goal
Broken, worn out, clapped out	Is not going to set the world on fire	The best quality available
Makes you feel poor	Feels neutral	Makes you feel incredibly abundant

Go through your life and possessions and categorize each section using the table above as a guide. Remember, this is according to your own personal standards and how it makes you feel. There are no right or wrong answers.

2. Highlight all the luxury areas in your life. In the example below, the luxury areas are Liz Earle skin-care products and Swarovski pen.

Area	Possession	Description	Class
Bedroom	Bedding	White sheets	Average
Bathroom	Skin-care products	Liz Earle	Luxury
Handbag and contents	Pen	Beautiful Swarovski purple pen	Luxury

Close your eyes and step into that space of abundance, luxury and prosperity. Use visual images, colors, smells, sounds, tastes and sensations to describe how you feel when you use each of these things. Stay in that space for a few minutes, pressing the tip of your middle finger against the tip of your thumb on both hands. This will anchor these positive feelings.

Come back into your current space and write how you feel using your luxury items (in this case a favorite notebook and pen).

3. Look at the areas of your life that you feel need improvement and come up with one small step that would make you feel more abundant.

4. Identify areas and items to be decluttered. I like to use the "5 F's" method. If it does not fit, flatter, function, fill you with joy, then fling it out. Take immediate action and start the decluttering today.

5. Whenever you feel a lack mentality or feel yourself slipping back into poverty consciousness, look at all the areas of your life that you have identified as being luxury and press your middle finger against your thumb to anchor in those positive feelings.

Redo this exercise once every few months or as often as necessary, and journal your progress in your favorite notebook.

Here are some examples of clients that used this exercise:

Mary C did this exercise and realized that her bathroom towels were ancient and had holes in them. She did not even like the color but they functioned and she felt it would be wasteful to get new ones.

When she saw a sale in a local department store she immediately ordered a new set of beautiful, soft, fluffy towels in the color she wanted, at an affordable price. She gave the old ones to an animal shelter and felt abundant because she was able to give and receive.

This small action was a turning point in Mary's life. She made a conscious decision not to settle for less than she felt she was worth. Mary said "dust settles, I don't". Every morning, she would dry herself off with her beautiful towels. She would look in the mirror and say "this is what a wealthy woman looks like".

Because of this new, inner confidence, Mary secured a promotion and a pay rise in her job.

Bill G was also experiencing a feeling of lack and scarcity. During this exercise, he realized that he absolutely loved his wallet. It had been a gift from his wife, it had his initials on it and this encouraged him to keep it tidy and organized. He felt it was a metaphor for how he felt about money. Every time he used the wallet it made him feel good about money.

Bill decided that he would always keep some paper money in his wallet so that he could never "run out" of money. This simple technique had a profound effect on his life. He felt his wallet was like a talisman and that he could never fail. Bill began to seek out more opportunities for his business that allowed him to almost double his income in a year.

Tips for coaches
This exercise may bring up some emotions and resistance. The purpose is not to make a client feel more shameful about lack but to remind them to focus on all the wonderful things already in their life.

Encourage the client to record daily all abundance that comes into their life. Whether it is in the form of money or a gift, it can be recorded on an abundance tracker, available from www.prudencemoneypenny.com/tracker or in a simple notebook. The method does not matter, the action does.

ACT ON YOUR VALUES AND MOVE TOWARDS THE LIFE YOU WANT

By Cecilia Olsson

This exercise helps you move toward a meaningful, vital and fulfilling life by discovering the values that lie underneath your goals. It's for anyone that wants to find greater motivation for healthy habits and behaviors so they can stick to goals that are important to them.

Great for:

- People who are stuck in unhealthy behavior patterns.
- People who can't change their habits but aren't sure why.
- People who want more motivation to make positive changes in their life.

Anyone that has tried to make a change in their lifestyle, such as a change of diet or starting to exercise, knows how difficult it can be to stick with it. You read tons of books on healthy foods and exercise but still find it difficult to actually get it done.

You start off feeling super inspired but within the first few weeks, or when facing challenges, the inspiration tends to wear off. However, there are a good few things that can help you along the way when you want to change your life.
I´ll guide you through one of my favorite exercises to help you get where you want to go.

Step 1: Find out the value behind the change you want to make
Why is it important to you? Now, I want you to take a really good look at this and question whatever comes up first. If your answer is "I want to look good on the beach", think again. Is this so important you´d like to have it engraved on

your tombstone? "Cecilia was the kind of woman who always looked good on the beach"? Probably not.

What's the deeper value behind it? To take good care of your health? Because you want to have enough energy to play with your kids or grandchildren? It is important to find the deeper value behind the change as this will keep you motivated when you face challenges. Express your values in terms that make them everlasting, something you can always do more of. For e.g. being a loving and supportive partner is something you always can do more of, as it never gets finished, and this will keep your motivation going.

Step 2: Observe what brings you closer to your values or further away
Now that you've found your value, I want you to imagine placing the value in front of you. It could be "I want to take better care of my health so that I'm able to do the things that are important to me" or "I´d like to be present, open and loving to myself and others so that I'm able to have the kind of relationships I want". Now start investigating your day-to-day behaviors. Observe yourself as you move through the day – what behaviors are bringing you closer to the value ahead of you and which ones are moving you further away?

Step 3: Identify what keeps you stuck in unhealthy behaviors
Acknowledge the behaviors that bring you closer to your values and ask yourself if you could do more of them. Once you've identified behaviors that are taking you away from your values, try to understand the function behind these behaviors. We behave in ways that give us quick gratification, and quite often it has a short term benefit. Often it's about getting relief from difficult thoughts and emotions, like "I don't have what it takes" or "I can't stand this craving of cigarettes or chocolate" or "If I say no, they won't like me". This takes some radical self-honesty, and it might not always be pretty. To be totally honest about your behaviors is the best and quickest way

to find out what keeps you stuck. It will help you understand why you keep doing things that are taking you further away from the life you want! Please be assured–you are in good company! We all use unhelpful strategies to handle life from time to time.

Step 4: Find new ways to relate to your behavior
Now that you've identified what's keeping you stuck, try to find ways to relate to the situation that will help you take a step towards your values. It could be "I'll commit to taking a small pause before I say yes to things to make sure it's something I want to do, and I'll give myself permission to say no if it's not". If you eat for comfort, how can you comfort yourself in other ways, could you maybe call a friend? If you drink alcohol to unwind, how can you unwind in other, more healthy ways? Use your values and set a goal that is in line with those values. For instance, if I've set the goal to lose xx kilos and the value behind it is to take better care of myself so that I'm able to do the things I want, jumping on an extreme diet that makes you starve is not going to be in line with your value. Remember, no matter how small a step might seem, you are moving towards the life that you want.

Step 5: Practice self-compassion
Treat yourself with love and care. Let's say you find out you use food to dull the emotion of shame in step 3. Suddenly you find yourself having finished a big bowl of ice-cream that you did not intend to eat and you get really upset with yourself. What emotion is likely to show up? Shame. And what is your pattern of dealing with shame? To eat. So what is likely to happen next? That's right, you eat something else to dull this pang of shame (probably accompanied with a never-ending stream of thoughts telling yourself that you are useless, that you knew this would happen and that you might as well give up). Your tender love and care for yourself will really make a huge difference in you making progress.

Tips for coaches

If you are using this exercise with a client you want to give them time and space to process each step. There might be some resistance as you move through the steps as you need to take a close look at the very thing the client wants to avoid. I find the dentist metaphor useful here – if you go to the dentist to get help with a toothache, the dentist needs to see the tooth that's hurting. It's the same thing here, I need to see where it hurts to be able to help you with your pain and struggles.

WHAT WOULD MY HORIZON SELF DO? ACCOMPLISH GOALS BEING THE BEST VERSION OF YOU

By Nik Wood

This exercise will help you connect with and embody your horizon self, the version of you that will help you accomplish your goals. It will assist you in developing new patterns of thought and behavior that are aligned with who you want to be. This exercise is for anyone that needs to personify specific qualities in order to find the success they desire.

Great for:

- People that have a big goal but are have difficulty doing what it takes to reach it.
- People that need help overcoming a challenge or a problem.
- People that want to tap into new personality traits to accomplish their goals.

— — —

Have you ever wished that someone else could magically step into your body and take over during those pivotal moments of your life when it really counts? Here's an exercise to unstick you and connect you to the exact version of yourself that you would need to be to move powerfully towards your most important goals. I call this your Horizon Self.

When I was a kid I loved the TV show *Quantum Leap*. It was the story of brilliant scientist Sam Beckett who theorized that time travel was possible inside his own lifetime and stepped into something called the "quantum leap accelerator" and vanished. What happened was that his consciousness was thrust back in time into other people's bodies, into other people's lives.

It turned out that Sam always jumped into the body of someone who was in a pivotal moment in their life. It was then up to him to change the past (space-time continuum be damned!) by taking some action that these people could not take on their own.

I have certainly had moments of my life where I wished that someone could jump into my body and set some things right. One day I noticed something about that line of thinking which led to many breakthroughs and to this exercise. What I noticed was that there was a part of me that believed that the right person could step into my life and achieve the great things that I didn't believe I could achieve on my own.

Prior to this thought I had been buying into a story that said I didn't have what I wanted in life because I didn't have enough of something. Not enough money, time, energy, support, etc. Believing that someone could step into my life, into my circumstances, and just through having a different perspective and some other skills or experiences, accomplish what I could not meant that I had to drop those other excuses.

Once I dropped into this realization I was able to fully get what Tony Robbins says "It's not the lack of resources, (but rather) it's your lack of resourcefulness that stops you." I imagined that if I were to drop Tony Robbins into my body, in my life, that he'd be a millionaire impacting countless people by the end of the month. I imagined that if I were to drop four-time CrossFit Games winner Rich Froning into my body and my life that I would be on my way to a much higher fitness level by the end of the month.

If these things were true (they felt true) and using someone else's mindset could help me better achieve my dreams from my current position in life, then perhaps all I needed to do was change my own mindset.

This is not a new thought but seeing it from this angle made it feel new to me. The thing was, it's one thing to believe that someone else can do the things we dream of, it's another thing to see ourselves as capable of reaching our dreams, especially if we don't have any sort of track record that allows that kind of belief in ourselves.

I realized that it would be more empowering to shift my mindset by imagining the best version of me rather than visualizing someone else stepping into my body. So I asked myself, "Who is the version of me that could powerfully handle the challenge in front of me?"

Imagining an infinite set of realities where versions of you have gone down every conceivable path and played every available role is a fun mental exercise that allows this exercise to help you achieve your goals. If you can imagine the you who not only could, but already has, overcome the challenges you are currently facing, you can have them "Quantum Leap" into your current reality and take care of your challenge or goal. If you can imagine a version of you who has developed into the person who took your life and turned it into the life of your dreams, then you can imagine yourself doing it now too.

So here is how to tap into your Horizon Self and get them working for you now.

Firstly, imagine a time beyond the successful completion of the challenge in front of you. If your current challenge is tied to a larger one, imagine having that larger challenge successfully completed.

Complete the following prompts in order as thoroughly as you need:

1. "If this challenge were already successfully dealt with I would have…":

(More money? Happiness? Love? Improved Fitness?)

2. "In order to get there I had to take these actions…"

(Write as many actions as you can think of and then put them in order from the next action you would have to take from the present moment, until that one immediately before completion. *Bonus points for TAKING that first action immediately after completing this exercise.)

3. "Having accomplished this goal I got to be…"

(Who do you imagine you would be if you accomplished this goal? Would you be happier, more fulfilled, more calm, more grateful, and appreciative? Write it all down.)

4. "In order to have accomplished that goal I needed to be…"

(What traits would you have to take on in order to accomplish your goal? Would you need to be consistent, resilient, relaxed, playful, determined?)

So now what you have is a list of personality traits that you would need to be to move on the path towards your goals as well as the qualities that you would have when you achieved them. This is the description of your Horizon Self, the version of you who has already achieved what you want to achieve.
At this point it's important to breathe and take a moment to visualize your Horizon Self and choose. Will you allow this version to take over? Will you let go of the familiar and embrace a new way of doing things? If yes, then picture this more developed and experienced version of you joining forces with you to hit your Horizon Goals.

Now, it's up to you to embody the traits you've laid out and to bring those qualities to the actions you've listed. If you are being the person who can reach your goals and taking the actions that point you in their direction, you will be set up to reach your goals.

Just keep asking WWMHSD? (What Would MY Horizon Self Do?). Trust in them, trust in yourself, and act from that place. It's that simple.

RADICAL PRIORITIZATION: GET YOUR MOST IMPORTANT WORK DONE TODAY

By Donita Brown

Create the structure and accountability to accomplish what matters most to you, instead of just fighting fires every day. This exercise is for people who don't feel like they're accomplishing what is most important to them and who struggle with time management.

Great for:

- Working parents struggling to balance work and life.
- Professionals who are overwhelmed and drained at the end of the day.
- People who have a lot on their plate and need to manage their time carefully.

- - -

"What is important is seldom urgent and what is urgent is seldom important." Dwight D. Eisenhower

This exercise is for working professionals, such as busy moms and dads, new college graduates or those juggling going back to school while working full-time. Having chased the lie that a work-life balance is attainable, you've either tried to do everything and failed or have failed to do what matters most.

Being in control of how you spend your time is especially important when you feel you don't have time for everything you want to do. The problem is we tend to spend our time on urgent tasks and overlook the things that are truly important to us.

The Eisenhower Matrix pictured below, which I call here Radical Prioritization, is a time management tool that can be used to group your tasks according to how important and urgent they are.

160

Urgent tasks demand immediate attention, and if we're not careful, the urgent items can consume the whole day. This could be dealing with a health issue that could have been avoided with healthier habits or not planning well and running late on deadlines.

Important tasks help us achieve life goals. This is why it is essential to keep your eye on what is most important to you. If you spend your time accomplishing tasks that are not in line with what is important to you, you will finish the day exhausted and frazzled.

Important tasks are where we should be spending our time. These can include getting enough rest, spending quality time with family, helping your children with homework, saving money by cooking at home, and working with high performers on your team. Important tasks fall into two categories - "Urgent & Important" or "Not Urgent & Important".

Eisenhower Matrix

RADICAL PRIORITIZATION

URGENT & IMPORTANT –
QUADRANT 1

- ☐ _____
- ☐ _____
- ☐ _____

IMPORTANT, NOT URGENT –
QUADRANT 2

- ☐ _____
- ☐ _____
- ☐ _____

URGENT, NOT IMPORTANT –
QUADRANT 3

- ☐ _____
- ☐ _____
- ☐ _____

NOT URGENT & NOT IMPORTANT –
QUADRANT 4

- ☐ _____
- ☐ _____
- ☐ _____

DONITABROWN.COM

This exercise helps you to create the structure and accountability in your daily schedule so you accomplish what matters most to you, instead of just fighting fires every day.

Step 1: Categorize the importance and urgency of your tasks

1. Urgent & Important tasks
Write down 3 things that you find yourself doing every day because you are reacting to situations. These are tasks which must be done today, but often could have been avoided with a little bit of planning. For example, today I had to make sure my children had clean uniforms for school.

If you're not careful, these tasks will consume your whole day.

The goal is to look at these tasks with a critical eye. What could have been done to avoid this urgency? For me, I could have bought more uniforms (a "Not Urgent & Important" task) so I didn't have to do laundry mid-week.

2. Not Urgent & Important tasks
Write down 3 things that you would really like to do and are important to you. For me this list includes: writing a book, getting a morning walk in daily, and reading daily.

3. Urgent & Unimportant tasks
Write down 3 things you did today or yesterday which came up and had to be attended to, but someone else could have done, either delegated or hired out to a service like Fiverr. For example, yesterday I could have got one of the people on my work team to prepare an agenda for that meeting.

4. Not Urgent & Unimportant tasks
Write down 3 things you did today or yesterday that could have waited. Be careful here to not put something in this category which is actually important. For example, today for me this was planning a trip happening much later in the year, packing

the car even though my husband agreed to do it and getting sucked into a Facebook Group on hiking.

Step 2: Create a new schedule using your priorities

Most people spend most of their time on Urgent tasks, which means they neglect the Important ones. When we do not prioritize correctly, we find that our time is used by others.

Here's how to change your schedule so you spend more time on the things that are important to you:

1. Be deliberate about your daily choices

If tomorrow it is important to be engaged in a long meeting, is it more important for you to sleep and be rested or wake up early and take a morning walk? It's a choice that is personal but you can't make this choice without a little bit of planning.

Before you go to bed, write down your schedule for the next day.

Think about and write down the time you will get up, the time you will leave the house and so on. Think about what you will do for each hour of the day. Be purposeful about your daily choices.

2. Re-write your task matrix daily

If you know you have one thing that is critical to do, then put it in the Urgent and Important quadrant. Think through what is required. Is it vital that you have lunch with your daughter or call your sister? If you've made your schedule, you'll know what time you have available and the trade-offs you are making with your time. This schedule will help you stay accountable to the actual amount of time you have to do tasks.

If, for example, you are going to be at your son's ballgame all day, then you most likely cannot spend time writing out a business case which often takes all day, so you'll have to move that to a different place on your matrix. If this business case is critical, then how are you going to get it done? What trade-offs are you willing to make? Consider that while this may be Important, it may not be Urgent and can wait until tomorrow or the next day.

Keep your Matrix with you, and review it 2-3 times during the day. Use an Evernote template to keep it online, or simply write it down each day on a sheet of paper.

Tips for coaches
As a coach, it is your job to help your client think through the urgent and important items. An excellent way to do this is to have them keep track of the number of Urgent and Important tasks they have in a week. Your goal is to help them reduce the number of "Urgent & Important" tasks to 1-3 a week (not a day!). Emergencies happen but they should not happen every day.

NEW MOON VISION BOARD INTENTION SETTING

By Christine Compas

This exercise helps you get clear on the intentions you wish to manifest in your life, while channeling the powerful manifestation energy of the New Moon to plant and grow these new seeds in your life! It's for entrepreneurs or anyone looking to accomplish important goals in their life.

Great for:

- People who need more clarity on their goals.
- People who wish to manifest a certain feeling within their life.
- People who want to continuously achieve new objectives.
- People who want to align their goal setting with the universal flow of energy.

— — —

You may be aware that there is natural flow of energy within our Universe, and the more we are able to align our lives with that natural flow, the easier life becomes. This exercise is one of the ways that I have found I have been able to tap into the natural flow of energy and use it to my advantage to manifest the things that I seek in life with great ease and speed.

This exercise has three elements to it: the power of the moon, astrological insights, and visualization.

1). The Moon
Ceremonies honoring the power of the moon's phases can be found in almost every ancient civilization. Traditionally, the New Moon has been honored as the best time for starting new projects, planting seeds, or for new beginnings. For this reason, the New Moon is the best day of the month to set a new intention.

2). Astrology

Each of the twelve zodiac signs carry with them certain energies and qualities. An Aries, for example, is a Fire sign that has been dubbed "The Warrior" for their bold and courageous attitude in life. Whenever we are in Aries season (March 21 – April 19), we all have the ability to tap into our inner bold and courageous selves with greater ease, no matter what our own sign is.

In the case of this exercise, you can use the power of the zodiac sign that the New Moon falls within, in order to channel that sign's energy into your intentions. Another approach is for your intention to match the element of the sign. For example, Aries is a Fire sign, and Fire signs are known for having great passion, so when you are thinking of your intention for the New Moon in Aries, you could also think about what you wish to bring more passion to within your life.

3). Visualization

By creating a vision board with your intentions on it, and placing it in a location where you will see it regularly, you are subliminally programming your mind to keep your intentions or goals at the forefront of your attention. Whenever the Universe puts something in your path that might help you in achieving that intention, you are much more likely to notice it.

Steps

1. As the next New Moon approaches, take some time to find out what astrological sign we are currently in. Once you find that, look up a few qualities about that particular sign, as well as its element (Air, Fire, Earth, or Water). Then, take some time to think about what area of your life could use an infusion of that type of energy in it.
2. In order to utilize the planting power of the New Moon, it is best to set your intention and create your vision board on that day. However, if that is not an option, you can still harness that power for 48 hours both before and after the New Moon.

3. Intentions are not to-do lists or goals for external achievements and material possessions. Your intention is about how you want to feel when you achieve your vision or goal (e.g. hope, faith, certainty, trust, love, joy, peace, etc.).
4. Set a time frame for the goal/vision you are wanting to achieve. It can be any amount of time – 1, 3 or 6 months, 1 year, etc. If you really want to tap into the moon phase powers, I would suggest setting a 6-month time frame, as that's when we will have a Full Moon in that same sign. However, some intentions or goals may simply be on a longer or shorter time frame, so there is really no wrong or right length of time.
5. Take a poster board (I recommend using a corrugated or foam board) and create a vision of your intention/goal. You can then surround it with supporting mantras. (For instance if your intention is to be more calm at work, you could write "I react calmly to all situations.") Make it aesthetically pleasing so you will enjoy looking at it each day.
6. When you are finished, put your board in a place where you will see it every day. The more you see the board, the more you will focus on the goals and visions that it contains, and the more you will notice when the Universe is sending you things to help you.
7. Lastly, have fun with it! There is no wrong way to do a vision board.

Case study

Two years ago I was in the process of looking for a house. It was a seller's market, houses were moving very quickly, and despite looking at 6 or 7 houses a week, I was having no luck finding a house that felt right. I was reading my monthly horoscope and it mentioned that it was a good time for me to set some new intentions and perhaps even create a vision board, so I decided to try it out. One day before the New Moon I flipped through home magazines, pulling out pictures of homes that resonated with me, and put it up in my bedroom

167

where I would wake up and see it every day.

Three weeks later my realtor and I went to a house whose listing had only included external pictures of the house. I did not have a lot of hope about what that meant for the interior of the house, but when I walked in the door I was pleasantly surprised. It had nice hardwood floors, 10 foot tall ceilings, and lots of bright light. It was an odd feeling, but the more I walked around the house the more I felt like it was mine.

When we walked into the next house I immediately knew that the previous house was the one that I wanted and I made an offer that day. When I got back to my apartment I glanced at my vision board and noticed something interesting. The home pictures that I had posted included tall ceilings, lots of natural light, and beautiful hardwood floors. I realized that having it in front me on that vision board helped me realize exactly what it was that I was looking for.

SELF-LEADERSHIP: AN EXERCISE TO CLARIFY YOUR VALUES

By Cynthia Moffatt

Leading a fulfilling life starts with discovering your values. Clarifying, articulating and aligning with them helps you design your purposeful path forward. Whether you're an individual seeking to take charge of your life, a parent or community/organizational leader seeking to have a positive impact on others, or a professional coach supporting a client in developing their unique leadership style, this exercise will bring the clarity required to live and work with greater ease, harmony, fulfillment and satisfaction.

Great for:

- Individuals asking "what's really important to me?" and "how do I want to live my life?"
- Millennials, Gen Ys or Gen Zs just finishing their education, or heading out on their own.
- Leaders who want to be successful and effective within organizations.
- Family or community leaders who want to be strong role models.

— — —

It is said, *"If we ever hope to be effective leaders of others, we must first seek to be effective leaders of ourselves."* To effectively self-lead, we must determine what we value most and what drives our decisions and actions.

This exercise will support you through a thought provoking, self-discovery process resulting in a better understanding and ability to articulate how you'd like to live and lead your life. With clarity, you can develop a plan for more intelligent and intentional participation in your life by honoring your values, as well as measuring and confirming how your actions and choices are aligned with them.

How do we actually do that? How do we become truer to our *being* and more intentional in our *doing*? We start by clarifying our values:

Step 1: Developing the long list
The most effective way to clarify values is to pull them from our experiences. Pre-established lists and values worksheets are readily available online and while many people are successful at using an existing set of values for this exercise, there is the risk of "choosing" your values versus creating them. Rather, let the following two exercises help you create your own long list of values.

1. Pivotal Moments
Use life experiences to reveal what you value. A peak experience or special brief moment(s) in time when life was especially good or rewarding is one way. With a special moment in mind, get curious and ask: *"What was the environment, what was happening, who was I with? What were the values showing up and being honored in that peak experience?"* Test the wording around the values, writing them down and looking for those that really resonate.

In tandem, consider moment(s) in time where you were unhappy, angry or agitated. This method helps to identify values that are being overlooked or suppressed. The work here is to name the circumstance that caused the upset and reverse it to find the contradictory feeling or circumstance. Often times, we are able to best recognize a value when something gets in its way, so this process proves equally useful.

2. Pleasure and Pain Points
Look for areas in your life where you find ease and fulfillment. This is a sign of your values being honored as you'll bring the behaviors of order and organization naturally to things that are important to you. What conditions MUST you have in your life (e.g. a peaceful environment)? What MUST you do (e.g. be of service to others)? List the predominant value(s).

As you do this, also look for areas in your life where you see recurring gaps in satisfaction or actual pain points (e.g. feeling unfit, not making time for an important hobby); this is a sign of ignoring what you truly deem important. List the ignored or suppressed values.

Step 2: Developing the short list
As your values list takes shape, notice emerging patterns and repetition among words you've chosen. Group together and organize similar or related values and create a word, cluster of words or phrase that summarizes that group and is meaningful to you. (For example, if your list includes the words "education, improving, learning, challenge, etc." you may want to summarize these as "growth" or "challenge/growth".) This step will result in a shorter, more concise list of values for you while still capturing the essence and meaning of all your values.

Step 3: Prioritizing values
You will find many things important but you will also find some take precedence. Which values will you not compromise on? To create some hierarchy, with your shortened list from Step #2 above, consider how you would feel if:

a. Your current satisfaction level for each value was greatly *decreased*; and

b. There was a substantial *increase* in your satisfaction level with each value.

(For example, note whether you would be *excited, indifferent, devastated*, etc. by an increase or decrease.) From this reflection, you should be able to prioritize your top 3-5. These are your guideposts – things you deeply care about and want to focus action around.

Step 4: Connecting your values to action
Our values are either present or absent in the choices we make each day. Each of us are faced with thousands of choices daily; certainly, hundreds of key decisions that move us to action. Additionally, much of what gets decided or chosen is

habitual or routine in nature meaning we're less mindful about these choices. We act either out of habit, practice or a simple default to social ideals, tradition or pressure from others' wants instead of personal wants. In other words, many of us stumble into a life, a relationship, or a career versus intentionally and mindfully leading ourselves based on a value system we have become very clear about and have chosen to live from.

In this final step you create objectives to become more intentional in both your "being" and "doing". Objectives are intentionally broad. However, we don't live or work in the broad, big picture and to create change we must also have a plan of action. The worksheet below will help you accomplish this:

- Column 1: identify objectives, ideally not more than 3.
- Column 2: identify what you want – the goal required to meet your objective.
- Column 3: identify how to reach your goal – the action and/or behavior required to achieve it and which you commit to.
- Column 4: identify why you want to create change – the values which support your goals and those you can leverage.

Example:

OBJECTIVE	WHAT DO I WANT TO HAPPEN? WHAT DO I WANT TO CHANGE? (GOAL) (THE "WHAT")	HOW WILL I MAKE IT HAPPEN? WHAT WILL I DO ABOUT IT? (ACTION/BEHAVIOR) (THE "HOW")	WHY IS THIS IMPORTANT? WHAT CAN I LEVERAGE TO ENSURE MY SUCCESS? (VALUE) (THE "WHY")
Serve and share gained wisdom through writing and publishing a book.	• I want to spend more time alone writing and focusing on finishing my book. • I want an inspiring space from which to create. • I want to stop procrastinating and feel a sense of accomplishment.	• I will create a quiet space where I can focus on all aspects of getting the book written and published. • I will commit 4 hours each day to the writing process. • I will not beat myself up if I have an unproductive writing day. All experience serves the final product. • I will attend the Spring 2019 writers conference. • I will target Sept. 2020 as book release.	Values to honor and leverage: • Peaceful environment • Structure and systems • Compassion • Learning/Growth • Accomplishment • Service
Be explicit →	Include where, with whom, what achieving the goal might look, feel, sound like, etc.	Include specific behaviors and actions required; include a timeline, target dates, deadlines, etc.	Refer to your hierarchy of values and thoughtfully define why this is important to you.

Whether you complete this last step alone or with a professional coach, the practice is about fostering change (or perhaps transformation!) and connecting it to personal values to instill meaning for you. Remember, your values are the true and quiet forces behind your actions and decisions. Clarifying, and now including, your values in this very tangible way helps you realize the significant role they play.

Tips for coaches:
- Set aside at least two hours to deep dive into the process and allow space for questions, perspectives and good dialogue. An environment with plenty of natural light and a view to nature is conducive to helping clients quietly and thoughtfully reflect on the prompts in this exercise.
- It can be important to revisit this exercise with clients since personal values sometimes change over time. Even if there are no substantial changes to a client's values, re-clarifying is worthwhile in confirming the "rightness" of choices and decisions. Other values-based conversations expand this exercise, i.e., inquiring at any major decision point, *"Does this particular choice or action move you closer to or further away from what you value?"*

This exercise challenges you to lead and lead well, beginning with creating a life of purpose, contribution and service based on your values. It challenges you to confidently articulate and demonstrate going forward – *"This is who I am. This is important to me. This is how I live and work."*

STICK YOUR LINE LIKE A PRO: USING THE POWER OF STORY TO PROPEL YOUR GOALS

By Paul Kuthe

Accomplish your biggest goals! This exercise helps you increase your clarity, intrinsic motivation, accountability, and action toward your deepest aspirations. It's for elite performers, coaches, leaders, managers and mentors who want to help people do and achieve more.

Great for:

- Professionals who want to make a high stakes move in life or business.
- People who need to "try their goals on" for the right fit to renew their focus.
- People who are fearful of sharing their goals but want accountability.
- Coaches that want to establish a clear end goal in mind with their clients.

As I glide toward the next horizon line, the overhanging moss covered canyon walls tower far above. I can see the mist rising from the depths below with only the treetops visible just downstream. There is only one way out. The nearly deafening guttural roar of the river seems to make the surrounding trees tremble, or is that just my stomach? Sitting on the riverbank at the lip of the towering drop, anticipation courses through me as I make an effort to see my intended path amongst the chaos. I close my eyes…

At the highest levels of sport, athletes and coaches have long been harnessing the power of the human mind for elite performance. We often hear about athletes visualizing their moves and outcomes before they compete. Years ago, as a wilderness guide and action sport coach, I started having my athletes run training sessions in their minds. They would "practice" sticking the moves they needed to win, or simply survive.

Today, we take concepts and techniques from the world of extreme sports and apply them to business, transforming the careers of our clients. Running a waterfall and running a business require many of the same abilities. Both take commitment, courage, and an unrelenting drive to succeed no matter what. When the stakes are this high, it helps to be crystal clear on where you would like to end up.

Let's face it...traditional goal setting doesn't work. Creating a list of disjointed, vague aspirations doesn't engage others or create accountability. Most often we make goals, then set them aside and go about doing things the way we always have.

We make decisions based on emotion. A bullet list simply doesn't inspire action like a good story does. It doesn't reach us on an emotional level, therefore isn't memorable and it certainly isn't worth sharing with others. The human mind has evolved to process and learn through the art of storytelling. Our survival has long depended on our ability to do so.

By creating something the human brain engages with, you create the potential for action. It makes your goals worth sharing with others and creates clarity for yourself, greatly increasing your likelihood of success. In the hard times, when you get knocked off your line, returning to your story gives you the resilience and the grit to keep in the flow.

Having picked my route, it's time to take action. Sliding into the cool churning waters above the drop, I return to the goal in my mind. With clarity and purpose, I pull hard on the paddle, propelling myself into the main flow of the water. Time slows as the world falls away from under the worn hull of my kayak. Sticking the landing, I paddle away from the base of the drop beaming with pride, feeling a sense of accomplishment and bellowing a victory howl.

175

Steps

Use these 3 steps to "stick your line" and turn your goal story into reality!

1. Identify your goals
Identify some goals that you'd like to achieve over the next year that fit the SMART formula. Make them Specific, Measurable, Actionable, Realistic and Time based. Be sure to include a couple of personal goals and professional goals.

2. Tell a story (here's where things get really interesting...)
Create a compelling story around your goals. Write about a moment in the future you're experiencing as though it's happening right now and pulls together each of the goals into one moment. Be sure to incorporate all 5 senses. Really put yourself there and describe the sensations. Write it from a first person perspective, like I did with my example of kayaking. Integrate each of your goals into one fulfilling story.

3. Share your story
Now we take SMART and add three more letters making it "SMARTERS"
The "ERS" stand for Exciting, wRitten as a story, and Shared. Once your goal story is really exciting to you, it's time to share it with those you respect and wouldn't want to disappoint. By sharing your story you create personal accountability while allowing others in to help you achieve your dreams. When you are sharing it, be sure to select wisely. Not everyone in your social circle or family will be supportive and helpful in achieving your goal, even if they are well intentioned.

4. Take action
Be sure that everything in your story is actionable. The greatest risk with this exercise is you can actually fail to take action because you've already had a taste of what it is like to be there already, yet there is still work to be done. Be sure to build a plan around the goal with some easy wins that are

achievable right away to get the momentum going. After all, "a goal without a plan is just a wish."

It's important you appreciate and enjoy the work it's going to take to get there. If you get stuck and can't come up with a story, it's usually because you fear choosing and therefore missing out on other possibilities. Remember you can change it if something better comes along. It's your story.

Tips for coaches and leaders
This process can help reveal an employee or client's "why" and what truly motivates them. It's a great tool for strategic planning with a business owner and can be used at team building retreats. It can also help bring partners together toward a common goal or reveal how to help an employee toward their actual end goal.

This powerful exercise can be self-completed by a client or employee once the format is explained and an example story is shared. Because it demonstrates congruence, it's especially useful if the coach or leader shares their own personal goal story with the clients as the example. Once they have crafted a great story have them stand and read it out loud (just be sure to have some tissues ready as this can get emotional). You can also take this one step farther and have them create a visual representation on a vision board with the story at the center and then hang the board somewhere it can be seen daily.

THE PERSONAL QUARTERLY REVIEW

By Orian Marx

The Personal Quarterly Review provides a framework for deep self-reflection on your progress towards achieving your meaningful goals. It's particularly helpful for individuals who feel stuck, or those who feel overwhelmed by everything on their plate.

Great for:

- People who feels like they are stuck making progress in their life.
- People who feel like they might not be capable of tackling challenges that are pressing right now.
- People who feel overwhelmed by the number of things they are trying to handle concurrently.

These days people are busier than ever before. Feeling anxious and overwhelmed is a persistent problem for many. In our constant quest for getting things done, we forget to make space for acknowledging progress we've already made. We spend too much energy thinking "look how far I have to go" and not enough on "look how far I've come".

Conducting a personal quarterly review is a powerful method for building your confidence and clarifying your priorities over time, especially when combined with an annual goal setting process.

Consider that publicly traded companies all around the world are required to file quarterly reports - updating investors on their achievements and setbacks, and revising their future outlooks. This quarterly process is one of the main mechanisms by which companies and their investors measure progress and identify challenges.

The questions below provide a framework for you as the primary investor in your own life to reflect on your progress and recalibrate your efforts. Doing this every three months provides an increment of time that is long enough to provide for meaningful progress on goals, but not so long that you forget what's happened. It reduces anxiety and overwhelm by creating space to acknowledge your progress and achievement, while also allowing time to make reasonable adjustments for things that aren't working.

Steps

In an environment where you can be comfortable and focused for an hour or two, write down your answers to the following questions. You might write them as a series of bullet points or a stream of consciousness. You can write as much or as little as you like, but don't avoid writing something because it might seem insignificant to someone else. Unlike public companies, your quarterly reviews are for your eyes only (unless of course you want to share them with loved ones, or on social media - which is something I do and have found tremendous added benefit from).

Over the last three months...

Q1. What were my accomplishments?

List anything that feels like an accomplishment *to you* or that you want to recognize yourself for. (e.g. "finished writing my book", "enrolled in an improv class")

Q2. What helped me achieve these accomplishments?

List any motivations, tools, people, experiences, etc. that helped you make things happen. (e.g. "my spouse who never gives up on me", "writing my daily to-do list out on a separate sheet of paper")

Q3. What did I not accomplish that I intended to?

List anything you specifically thought would happen in the past three months that didn't. (e.g. "I didn't finish unpacking all the boxes", "I didn't ask for a raise")

Q4. What stopped me?

Describe any thought patterns or circumstances that you feel hindered you. (e.g. "I didn't think anyone would take me seriously", "I got sick")

Q5. What have I learned?

What lessons can you take away from the last three months? What new thoughts are present? (e.g. "I'm a lot more capable than I thought!")

Over the next three months...

Q6. What is one big thing I can accomplish that will make a meaningful difference in my life?

Choose one goal that you can reasonably accomplish in the next three months that would be a big deal for you. (e.g. "start a blog", "call my dad")

Q7. What do I want to start doing/do more of/do less of/stop doing?

List anything you want to work on in the next three months. (e.g. "start meditating", "go dancing every week instead of once a month", "spend less time on social media", "stop replying to negative comments on my blog")

Q8. What beliefs/values/motivations do I have that will help me achieve these goals?

What internal drives can you leverage in pursuing your goals? (e.g. Beliefs: "Making money enables me to make a bigger contribution to the causes I care about", "I am a reliable partner"; Values: "I am committed to producing excellent work, no matter what I'm working on", "I don't want to cause harm to animals"; Motivations: "I want to have freedom to travel the world", "I must leave this planet healthier for my children")

Q9. What other resources can I use to help me achieve these goals?

What external resources are available to you to help you pursue your goals? (e.g. "I have friends who are experienced entrepreneurs who could give me advice", "I can sign up for an online course in marketing")

Tips for coaches
Clients should be encouraged to feel unconstrained in answering these questions, as there are no "right" answers. The exercise is designed to generate new insights into what is meaningful and available to your client, so a certain amount of brainstorming should be encouraged. It is important to encourage your client to observe "small" accomplishments in addition to "big" ones.

This exercise is particularly effective as a guided group workshop, where individuals can be encouraged to share their answers with each other and offer resources for achieving future goals.

For more resources on this exercise, visit:
http://www.artoflifecrafting.com/activateyourlife

HOW TO MASTER ANY SKILL IN 100 HOURS

By Erik Hamre

This exercise helps you master a new skill in just 100 hours. You'll learn how to use 100 hours efficiently to optimize your time so you improve at a much quicker rate. It's for anyone who has an adventurous spirit, likes to learn or has ambitious goals and big dreams.

Great for:

- People who want to be able to master a new skill.
- People who want to learn a new skill in order to accomplish a goal or dream.
- People interested in personal growth and development.

\- \- \-

To have skill is to perform a particular activity very well, with accuracy, speed and a low number of errors. Unfortunately, you cannot completely master any new skill in 100 hours (or ever, as there is rarely an upper limit to performance). You can however achieve spectacular improvements with 100 hours of practice, and the experience may even redefine you as a person.

Skills define who we are, and in many cases how well we do in life. Having more skills makes it easier to meet and connect with people, and being good at something gives you a sense of pride and well-being. Developing skills also makes you more complex and interesting.

I've been researching and applying skill development research for the last 5 years. This year my goal has been to improve as much as possible at 10 different skills for 100 hours each (some of the skills I've been working on lately: piano, Portuguese, drawing, cooking, kizomba, chess, Thai massage, filmmaking, yoga, ultimate frisbee, asking good questions). And each time I've finished 100 hours of practicing a skill, I've become a noticeably changed person, thinking about the world in a whole new way.

Learning any skill is a bit like learning a new language. After you improve your drawing skills, you look at the world and think about how you would draw it, the shadows objects are casting, basic shapes and how things are overlapping. After improving your cooking skills, you have a different relationship with food, and when you are walking through a market you are constantly thinking of tastes and how they could fit together in a dish. Through dancing you learn a whole new way of communicating and connecting with the use of your body.

The key to fast improvement is to focus on performing every action as precisely as possible, but to also be aware of mistakes you are making, so that you can find ways to resolve them. When you consistently apply these principles for many hours of practice, your performance will steadily grow to impressive levels.

When learning a new skill these are the key principles you need to apply:

Quality of your attention
Be present when you learn any skill, and pay attention to what you are doing right now. Always pay full attention to the details that affect your performance.

For example, if you are learning a physical skill, perform every movement as well as you can. Your body doesn't know what you are trying to teach it. By moving in the correct way, your body will learn the best movement patterns faster. In the beginning, practice slower, but with high accuracy. When you start to perform the move well, increase the speed. But always keep the quality of movement, otherwise you will only improve at performing a move in a sub-optimal way.

Keep practicing. Don't just practice until you get it right once, practice until you can't get it wrong. Not until then have you fully learned the skill. If you are throwing a frisbee, see if you are able to do 5, 10 or 20 good passes in a row. Then try to perform the pass under more difficult conditions (under pressure from an opponent, in windy conditions, or from a lower/higher release point).

Energy management
To fully devote your attention to learning a new skill requires a lot of energy. The more energy you have at your disposal, the more potential practice time you have. Manage your physical and mental fitness and practice when your body and mind are rested. Only then are you able to focus 100 percent, and perform at the edge of your current abilities.

Take care to sleep well, eat nutritious food, stay hydrated, stay in shape and avoid situations that steal your energy. Plan your practice around the time of the day when you have the most energy.

Environment
Set up the environment to make it as easy as possible to practice. Prepare any equipment you need in advance and place it where you will easily see it. Limit distractions and barriers to practice. Live close to where you practice. Your goal is to make it as easy as possible to practice, to maximize the time you spend practicing and stretching your abilities, rather than spending your energy thinking about where, when and if you should practice.

Measurement
Find a way to measure your practice. I keep this part simple. Whenever I put in an hour of quality practice, I give myself a cross (aiming to get to 100). If you didn't practice with good quality attention, give yourself less (e.g. half a cross). If the quality was very low, don't give yourself any crosses, and evaluate what you can do to improve your next practice. Make it a habit to always practice with high quality attention.

Consistency
After you have made it a habit to practice with quality, focus on consistency. Practice every day. By continually making small improvements over a long period, you will eventually get a lot better.

Prioritize
If this is a skill that matters to you, spend your most rested hours every day on it. Then build the other activities in your life around it.

Learn to learn
Knowing how to actively develop and grow a skill is a skill in itself. If you learn the process of becoming good at anything, you can apply it to any skill. The more time you invest in learning, the better you become at it. Accelerated learning experts train their learning muscles all the time. They therefore progress faster than most people, and achieve a more sophisticated level of mastery in a shorter time frame.

Find a hero
Identify expert performers at the skill you want to learn. Figure out what makes them good. Design your practice around learning how to do that yourself.

Get a coach, be a coach!
All world-class performers have coaches to help improve their game. Whatever it is you do, it is always possible to get better. A great coach will help you plan your practice, give feedback on how you are doing and push you to perform at the edge of your current abilities.

At the same time, be your own coach. Get creative in how you challenge yourself and plan practice to stretch your current abilities.

Exercise: Redefine yourself - The 100 Hour Challenge
If you want to live the life you want, you need to develop the skills that let you do so, one skill at a time.

Often the most valuable skills are those that are difficult to learn. Because they are difficult to learn, fewer are willing to put in the effort to develop them. Invest in yourself, by putting in the work to get good at the skills that matter for you.

I cannot think of any skill that I'm proud of, that I didn't put a lot of effort into. You can only become exceptional at something by putting in a lot of effort. Ordinary is not sexy. Be exceptional!

If you want any exercise in life to be transformational, you need to put considerable effort into it and challenge yourself in a way which makes you proud of the outcome. This goes for all the exercises in this book.

My challenge for you is simple, but not easy. Choose a skill that you would most like to improve, and put in 100 hours of quality practice, applying the principles of learning mentioned above. By taking action, you can redefine yourself and the direction your life is going, one skill at a time.

PART 5: SUCCESS AND BUSINESS

Success mindset - Confidence – Storytelling

OVERCOMING SOULCRASTINATION

By Ian Griffith

This is the wake-up call everyone needs to connect with who they are and what they want. This exercise gives you the toolkit you need to go after your soul's purpose like your life depended on it. It's for anyone who is letting life, people or activities distract them from going after their dreams. If you're soulcrastinating you need to read this right away. It's time to stand up for your dreams, no matter what.

Great for:

- People that have important dreams they haven't been prioritizing.
- People that don't want to feel regret later in life when it's too late to pursue their dreams.
- Coaches and entrepreneurs who are playing small and not going after what they feel called to do.

— — —

A man reached the end of his life, it was his last day, and he could feel his life slipping away. As he thought about his entire life, he had so many questions? Questions any of us would have in that situation.

Did I do what I was supposed to do?
Did I fulfill my life's purpose?
Did I give enough to my loved ones and to the world?

He realized that he had let "life" get in the way. When he looked back on his life as a whole, he saw how much of it he had wasted in futile pursuits. It was almost as if he would do anything he could to distract himself to his true purpose. And now, at the end of his life, he saw the dreams he had were not to be. Why, why had he not listened to his intuition, his inner voice, why had he not fought for the dreams he had in his youth? Over and over again he saw memories where he had compromised and justified putting off his true calling. Always bargaining, always telling himself stories to make himself feel better. "I'm not ready. I can do it later. I have plenty of time."

According to Bronnie Ware, author of *The Top Five Regrets of the Dying*, the number one regret of those who are at the end of their life is "I wish I'd had the courage to live a life true to myself, not the life others expected of me."

When you put off your dreams constantly, you are in a state of soulcrastination. Soulcrastination is defined as: "To delay or postpone one's soul purpose in life." The biggest reason everyone soulcrastinates, is because there is fear. The fear of failure and the fear of success, each result creates a dramatic change in life.

The other source of soulcrastination is a lack of deadlines. Each day is filled with deadlines for jobs, friends, families, and obligations to others. How many times are deadlines set up to go after one's soul purpose? For most, the answer is never. Life seems like it will continue forever and everyone tends to work on the urgent before the important.

The mind rationalizes that there is always more time. However, the postponement ends up taking a lifetime. Those looking back are often left wishing they had had a louder wake-up call so they could have gone after their dreams. Well consider yourself lucky.

TAKE THIS IS YOUR WAKE UP CALL!

It's time to move towards your purpose, you must have the courage to say yes to your life no matter what. You must soulcrastinate no more. It's time to step up and fight for your dreams. There is only one hero who can save you from the distractions of life. That hero is you. Your future greatness is dependent on you standing up for who you are meant to be.

So here is my question to you. What is the one thing in life you want most of all? If it was your last day, what would you have wanted more than anything?

The second question is, how can you make that dream so attractive that it pulls you immediately towards it?

The number one way to make your dreams more attractive is to focus on how your accomplishment can contribute to the world and the people you love. Your life is a gift. Countless others have given to you at some point in your life. There is nothing more fulfilling than knowing that in some way, you have added your special gift to this world and it enriched the lives of others.

Say your dream is to be a great speaker. Think not only of giving your best speech ever but of the people who will come up to you crying with inspiration. See how the lives you have touched have, in turn, brought that inspiration to others. You have created a ripple effect that moves forward and potentially can affect millions of lives. Your impact can make waves that rock this world till the end of time. If you allow it to.

Now think of what happens if you don't show up. All those beautiful cascading domino effects cease to exist. When you don't go after your dreams because you are afraid of failing. That is turning a blind eye to the truth. The most significant failure would always be not showing up for your true destiny at all.

It's time for you to let your soul know that you are going to serve its purpose.

Repeat the following three times, with intensity and emotion.

I AM MY HERO
THIS IS MY TIME
I WILL NOT BE DENIED
I STAND UP FOR MY DREAMS
I SAY YES TO MY LIFE

NO MATTER WHAT

If you do not know your soul's purpose yet, that is ok. However, it's time to make figuring this out a top priority. You have to do whatever it takes to figure out what your soul wants to accomplish. Here is a powerful exercise I give my clients to teach them how to listen for their purpose, or to pursue it even more.

1. For the next 10 days, ask yourself how you can serve your soul's purpose no matter what? As you go through your day, your intuition will speak to you. Make sure you write that down and go after it as if your life depends on it.

2. For the next 30 days, ask your higher purpose, or your God, or the Universe how you can serve its purpose. How can you contribute to life no matter what? Write down the answers you get and go after them with complete focus and determination.

As you go through the exercises above, you will notice this intuition becoming louder, as you are developing a relationship with your true inner self.

The other thing you will notice is that when you work in harmony with your true purpose, a tremendous about of extra energy and resourcefulness becomes available to you. Your body, mind, and spirit are working together, and that collaboration turns you into a superhero. You are the hero you have always been waiting for. You can save yourself and say yes to your soul's purpose no matter what.

HOW TO TELL YOUR STORY AND BUILD A CHARISMATIC BRAND

By Lisa Kniebe

This exercise helps you get clear on your business journey and build a personal brand based on your story. It's for solopreneurs, coaches, speakers and creative professionals who are struggling to tell their story and want to add personality to their messaging.

Great for:

- Authors and speakers who want to open with their story to engage their audience
- Entrepreneurs who are running an online business and need to build warmth, personality and connection
- Wellness practitioners who have a personal journey that's been pivotal to their business
- Mindful business owners who find it hard to speak about themselves at networking events

— — —

Telling your story allows you to own who you are, step into your power and ignite a spark in the hearts and minds of those who follow you. After all, your story is the reason you're here, so it makes sense to share it.

But… It's common to feel blocked when it comes to telling your story. *Why?* Because your story can create all sorts of insecurities around how much to reveal, the impact it'll have and how interesting is it (and hence how interesting are you?).

However, when you nail your story and speak from the heart it creates a powerful synergy with your audience, giving you the confidence to build a charismatic brand.

Steps

Telling your story with clarity and confidence means working on the narrative of you, where you came from, how you got here and what you've learned on the way. Luckily, there are 5 simple steps to pulling this together.

And it all begins with a mountain...

The mountain exercise guides your storytelling – it helps map your journey, build tension and allows you to share your transformation.

For the mountain exercise I want you to write in the past tense, looking back over your life to explain how you got to this point. Being too close to your own story is what makes it such a challenge to write. It helps if you imagine you are a *character* in this story and describe yourself in the 3ʳᵈ person (using she/he and her/him, not I and me).

5 simple steps to climb your story mountain:

1. Orientation
This part of your story is set in the past. Think back to a time before you were in the business you are in today. Now introduce yourself (the character) and orientate us to what life was like at this time.

    a. Who is this character?
    b. What does life look like for them?
    c. What are their hopes and dreams?

My example...*Introducing Lisa, a primary school teacher who was thriving on the pressure of a busy classroom, juggling family life with travel and professional development. She'd gone into teaching to find a job for life, after many career changes from nurse to recruitment agent and cake decorator! She was hoping that the classroom would be the answer to her dreams of settling down in a career.*

2. Build-up

This part of your story is exploring the build-up to change. It's where you share the first niggles of discontent with your life (personal or professional). It's here you set the scene for the problem and tell us when you noticed things changing. This may be an internal shift or an external event.

    a. When was it clear that change was afoot?
    b. Was there a catalyst that forced awareness to your discontent?
    c. What resistance was there to change? What fears?

My example...*Lisa started to feel restless in the classroom, but she buried that feeling deep down. She was afraid of letting her family down if she couldn't settle in this career. The catalyst came when a stranger at a BBQ asked her what she wanted for herself and she had no answer.*

3. Big decision

The heart of your story is built around the crossroads, where living with the problem becomes too much and you face a big decision to make it right. That big decision maybe resigning from your job, leaving an unhappy marriage or starting a side hustle. The decision isn't always to start a business, but it may have been the catalyst that set you on that path.

    a. What decision or choice was made?
    b. How did that change things?
    c. Who was a mentor or influencer?

My example...*Lisa left teaching to travel and rediscovered her passion for writing. As her trip came to an end she was at a crossroads, go back to teaching or begin again? She decided to take a leap of faith and making writing her future, and started her business.*

4. Resolution

Here's where you start to wrap things up. You're going to bring the story up to present time and show us how it all turned out. This should include what business you started, whether that's changed direction and how things have evolved for you.

   a. How did it work out?
   b. What fresh challenges did it bring?
   c. What surprises were there along the way?

My example...*Lisa is now 3 years into her entrepreneurial life and it's been full of surprises. Although she thought she'd left her nursing and teaching careers behind, it turned out she's drawn on these skills more than ever. Her natural empathy, intuitive style and incisive questioning helps her clients gain clarity and confidence in their business messaging.*

5. Transformation

When you reflect on how far you've come, what learnings have you taken away? Tell us about the transformation you've experienced on a personal and professional level.

   a. What are the learnings?
   b. How has this shaped or changed you?
   c. What do you stand for today?
   d. What is true for you, now and forever?

My example...*Lisa has learned to know herself better, to look for the answers within and to trust her judgment. She stands for gentle leadership, mindful communication and personal growth. She's more confident to step up and share her message with the world, having seen her ability to create transformational shifts for others. What is true for Lisa, now and always, is that knowing yourself is the starting point for any journey.*

Tips for applying this exercise

When starting the mountain exercise stay *curious, playful* and *creative* to help you gently unwrap the story you want to tell.

The exercise is best approached as a *"fun little thing to do with a glass of wine"*, rather than a *"must-do target"* for the week!

Here's some of the ways I get into the playful, curious zone:
- Sit on the floor, laptop on my legs
- Write by hand on butcher's paper using colored pens
- Go to a café, put headphones in and listen to my favorite tunes

It's completely normal for you to feel this is messy and disjointed to begin with. Don't judge your writing, this is the raw material that you'll shape and polish later on.

Tips for coaches

Clients often look for the BIG moments that define their journey, but it's the small stuff that will help them tell their story. This may be a *random question*, a *feeling* or an anxiety or a *realization*. These small moments always precede the big stuff and as a coach drawing this out is a key to making the mountain exercise a transformational experience.

For more resources on using storytelling to build your brand, go here:
https://stellapolaris.com.au/heres-how-to-tell-your-amazing-start-up-story-with-confidence-and-clarity/

SUCCESS PATTERNS BLUEPRINT: CREATE YOUR PERSONALIZED FRAMEWORK FOR REPEATABLE SUCCESS ANYTIME YOU WANT IT

By Derek Loudermilk

The Success Blueprint allows you to fully understand what leads to your greatest successes so that you can deconstruct and create a repeatable framework to use to ensure future challenges are a success. It also helps integrate your success into your psyche, which helps you feel confident. It's for entrepreneurs, athletes, people looking to advance their careers, scientists, politicians and anyone who wants to undertake big goals and complex challenges.

Great for:

- People who want everything they do to be a huge success
- People who want to play bigger but don't feel super confident
- People who want to understand the hidden gems in their own talents and skills

– – –

We were driving along a rolling country road in Arkansas, coming back to the lodge after a full day of rock climbing during one of my Adventure Quest trips. "Who wants to tell us the story of their greatest success?" I asked from the front seat. Our group was already in the habit of sharing wins and supporting each other, so the normal shyness about sharing our greatness was gone.

Over the next hour we heard stories of grand achievements from every person in the car: getting through a divorce, coaching a hockey team to the state championships, discovering a new species of virus in Yellowstone National Park, and becoming a stand up comedian.

We interviewed each other to find out more: What was easy for you about that? Where did you have to show up consistently? How did you keep going? When did you know you were going to succeed? We kept asking questions until we had a complete picture of someone's success.

After each person told their story, we had them highlight some of the key ingredients for their achievement. We also reflected back the things we were noticing about the other's stories: "I noticed how much time you spent preparing for each pre-game talk" or "I noticed that you seemed to maintain your calmness, even in really tough situations".

A few weeks later, I was on a podcast and the host asked me: "If you could write a letter to your younger self, what would you tell them?"

I said, "I would give my younger self the exact blueprint for every success that I have had – all the ingredients and the pattern that made them work. And I would give other examples of near successes that didn't work and what was missing in making them a success. That way I would bypass all the trial and error, and it would be a success blueprint personalized to me.

Each person's success blueprint will be different. My own success blueprint includes: hard deadlines, consistent visualization, a strong emotional attachment to the outcome, and having good mentorship along the way.

For others key factors might include: using your favorite talents, trusting in yourself, having family support, public acknowledgement, or a willingness to be uncomfortable.

Imagine if every time you started a project you could guarantee it would succeed and correctly identify all the places along the way where you might get stuck. You would never fail! You would have to be careful about what and how many things you start, because everything you try would succeed.

This is what you will experience if you create your personalized success blueprint. Here's how to do it:

Step 1: Your biggest successes
Pick your top three biggest long term successes and write down the story of each one. These can be in any area of life - from getting married, graduating college, running a 5K race, starting or selling a business, etc. It needs to be a "long term" success because these longer and more complex challenges are what ultimately lead to the greatest fulfillment. Long-term achievements rely less on luck and more on consistent implementation of skills – and therefore we can devise repeatable formulas for ourselves. Bonus points for telling the story out loud to friends or family and having them reflect back to you what they notice.

Ask yourself:

- What patterns are consistent between these successes?
- What was the biggest point of leverage in each story?
- What are the key skills you employed?
- Where did you create luck or good opportunities?
- When did things feel really easy?
- What outside people or events contributed to your success?
- What allowed you to take consistent action?
- Who were you being or how were you showing up at key moments?
- What were the conditions like in the rest of your life?
- What was your emotional connection to the project?

Step 2: Your biggest "not successes"
Write down the story of 1-3 "not successes". These will be efforts that could be anything from utter failures to things you have not completed or things that went moderately well, but could have gone way better. For myself I might include dropping out of my PhD program or launching a podcast only to stop a month later.

With these "not successes", you are looking for main difference between them and your big wins. Was there a key element missing? Examples here might include, not listening to your gut, relying too much on other people, not caring enough about the outcome, or not doing things you are good at.

Putting it into action
When you devise your goals and plan big projects, make sure you build in your personal conditions for success (in addition to your normal framework – like SMART goals). Maybe that means hiring a coach, setting financial consequences, getting a buddy, making a game out of it, doing something that feels easy or natural, or takes advantage of your greatest skills.

Bonus points for building in contingency plans for any of the patterns that show up in your "not successes". For example, if you failed because your previous effort relied too much on willpower, how can design the project differently to avoid needing to rely on willpower? Or if you need to work on a certain skill (sales, intuition, confidence, etc.), can you actively improve that until it doesn't hold you back?

ZONE OF CONFIDENCE: DISCOVER YOUR TRUE STRENGTHS AND CREATE EFFORTLESS SUCCESS

By Diane Hopkins

Zone of Confidence helps you identify your biggest strengths so you can create greater ease and fulfillment in your business and life. Once you really understand your natural gifts, and value them, you can write powerful books, give inspiring talks and create transformative programs that generate easier success for you. This exercise is for coaches and entrepreneurs that are ready to become thought leaders and impact bigger audiences.

Great for:

- People who aren't certain about what their biggest strengths and skills are.
- People who don't have the clarity or confidence to create their next big project.
- People who look at other's successes to decide what is best for their business.

– – –

We are often the last people to see our own strengths and we are usually the last people to value them. Knowing what you're good at and having the courage to apply those skills to everything you do is the key to success in life, especially if you're an entrepreneur or coach.

There are often so many new skills to learn that we forget to make it easier for ourselves by building what we're creating around our natural strengths – whether that's writing a book, creating a service or product, or deciding between starting a blog or a podcast.

When I start working with clients the first thing I usually notice is that they're not using their strongest skills in everything they do. They're often trying to "do it all" or are following what the leaders in their niche are doing. They're looking to the world outside to figure out what people want before they first look inside to see what they can best offer the world. As a result, they feel unsure about what to do next and lack the confidence to move forward with the new project they've been thinking about.

This cycle of ignoring our gifts leads to a lack of focus, being spread too thin and feeling dissatisfied as we spend time chasing projects that aren't really suited to us anyway.

Building our business around our strongest skills helps us make clever choices about what to create and it also tells us how we should market ourselves and get our message out there. It makes our work much more enjoyable and effortless, and gives us the resilience to keep going when we bump into obstacles.

Using our strengths gives us genuine confidence, not the "fake it until you make it" kind, that enables us to share our work with more ease and enthusiasm.

This exercise will help you identify your strengths so you can focus your energy on the right projects and deliver them in way that highlights your natural gifts.

Step 1: Review your strengths

Answer the following questions and get as specific as possible.

1. What positive things do people say about you and your work?

For e.g. *Your podcasts are fun to listen to. I feel like you really listen to me. I know exactly what I need to do after our coaching session. I really like the group of people you brought together in our mastermind.*

If you can't recall the positive things people have said, you may need to read over your client testimonials or ask for feedback from a few of your best clients or trusted peers.

2. What projects were the most successful for you?

For e.g. *My YouTube channel has a good following. That mastermind I ran last year got filled up quickly. I get a lot of referrals from my 1:1 clients.*

Think over the projects that have gone well for you in the past, in your current business or in previous jobs you've had.

3. What tasks do you find the easiest to do in your work?

For e.g. *Writing blogs is easy. Facilitating a group is simple. Coaching people 1:1 is easier than creating online content.*

It's important here to distinguish between tasks that you're good at because you've done them a lot and tasks that you do with genuine ease. For example, you may be trained as a 1:1 coach (so you're competent at it) but you may find facilitating groups easier.

4. What do you enjoy doing the most in your work?

For e.g. *I like making videos. I prefer interviewing people over writing blogs. I'd rather pre-record videos than do live group calls.*

It's important that your next project includes a lot of things that you enjoy doing (not just things that you're good at), otherwise you're likely to become resentful or procrastinate on getting it done. When you like what you're doing, you'll naturally bring more enthusiasm to it.

5. What recurring themes come up? What new insights do you have about your strengths?

E.g. I notice that the themes of interviewing people and working with groups keep coming up. I didn't realize how much I like making videos.

Now that you've identified your strengths it's time to put them together to discover your Zone of Confidence.

Step 2: Identify your Zone of Confidence

Your Zone of Confidence = Your *Skills* + Your *Personal Style* + Your *Impact*

Your *Skills* are the activities you've identified in Step 1 that you're good at doing. Examples: public speaking, facilitating groups, interviewing, editing videos, writing blogs.

Your *Personal Style* is the personality qualities that define how you naturally show up in your work. Examples: calm, down-to-earth, fun, authentic, energetic, inspiring, strategic, detailed.

Your *Impact* is what you do for other people to help them overcome their challenges and achieve their goals. Examples: motivating others to take action, helping people to be themselves, crafting simple strategies that are easy to implement.

1. Create a table like this in your journal or on your computer and fill in your own strengths. Be specific.

Skills	Personal Style	Impact
E.g. Interviewing	*Energetic*	*Motivating others to action*

This step is intended to help you spot your own strengths but also to value them properly. We often overlook and devalue the things that come easiest to us.

Step 3: Assess your current and future projects

The final step is to evaluate what you're currently doing with your business and decide on future projects that align closely with your strengths.

1. What should you keep doing? What current projects are closely aligned with your strengths? What do you need to let go of?

2. What should you do more of? What future projects are you considering that are best aligned with your strengths? What skills and qualities will you bring to these projects?

When you assess the projects you're working on you may discover that not everything is aligned with your core strengths.

One of my clients did this and we discovered that her two biggest strengths were showing up live on video and facilitating groups. Prior to that she had been trying to cover all her bases doing 1:1 coaching, group masterminds and online courses because that's what she had seen other successful coaches in her niche do. With this new insight she decided to let go of creating more online courses and focus on group masterminds and running retreats, where her biggest strengths would be best utilized.

Tip: Get feedback
It can be difficult to spot your own strengths and we usually need reassurance and validation from someone else before we feel really confident about what we do well. Get feedback from a coach or trusted peer, or collect surveys from a small group of your best clients. When you notice positive patterns of feedback you'll start believing in your natural gifts and you'll find the confidence to design everything you do around them. That's when life gets a lot more fun!

For more resources on using your strengths to share your work with bigger audiences, visit: http://www.wordandwing.co/activate

INTROVERTS: HARNESS THE POWER OF PASSION

By Lucinda Curran

This exercise helps you make difficult tasks achievable with ease, enthusiasm and without exhaustion. It's for introverted entrepreneurs who find they often need to perform tasks that take them right out of their comfort zone.

Great for:

- Introverted entrepreneurs
- Anyone needing to perform tasks that are quite a stretch out of their comfort zone
- People who are drained by public speaking and struggle with presentations.
- Business owners who seem to have lost their way or purpose

– – –

Many cultures highly value extroversion, and the world of business is no exception. As an entrepreneur, the challenges can be epic, especially when you are flying solo in your business. In this case, you will frequently be the brand, and this in itself is a tough place to be when you are an introvert. There are numerous tasks – like public speaking, team meetings, and planning sessions which can leave an introverted business owner feeling exhausted, overwhelmed and overstimulated.

The exercise that I am sharing is designed to help you manage these situations so that you can move through them with ease by creating a deepened connection to the uncomfortable task you need to do for your business. Most introverts find it extremely difficult to engage in something that lacks substance and has no meaning or purpose. By deeply connecting to the topic of the talk or the reason for the work, there is a greater sense of ease and the task becomes a step in contributing to the world in a meaningful way.

Getting to the core of why the work you do is important is a key to carrying out these comfort-zone-stretching tasks with ease. You can overcome your discomfort with the more difficult aspects of your work by recognizing the meaning of what you're doing, the part that gets you all fired up and the benefit for the greater good.

In short, appreciating that you are an introvert allows you to recognize your deep need to be involved in projects that are important to you, and this allows you to perform at a much higher level.

I was always a shy introvert and would turn as red as a beetroot if I needed to speak in front of a group. My chest would tighten and my voice would waver. Somehow I would get through, even though tears welled in my eyes and I felt so uncomfortable with everyone looking at me.

Since then, I have developed this technique which has enabled me to identify how the work I do is really important, that it is serving others and the planet. I've realized that my voice is needed in order to help others, and my mindset has totally shifted. The result? I have hosted radio shows, conducted 100's of interviews, delivered training all around the country, and become a keynote speaker at international conferences.

Steps

You can do this exercise alone, or with the guidance of your coach.

Identify one aspect of your business that is difficult for you. Write it down.

1. Close your eyes. Breathe. Think about this aspect of your work.

2. Where are your struggles? How does that feel? Where do you feel it?

Write or draw your answers. Or you may prefer to just visualize them. Either way, be sure to get a strong sense of how you react when you think about this task. Notice how your body responds, where you feel it, how intense the feelings are. See it, smell it, taste it, really experience it.

Breathe. Let it go.

3. Now think about *why* this aspect of your business matters. See the flow-on effect of you performing this. What happens next? Where does the benefit flow? How does this contribute to society or the world?

4. How does that feel? Where do you feel it?

Again, really feel and sense how your *why* makes you feel in your body.

Breathe. Hold this feeling of expansion. Smile.

5. Draw yourself completing this task with ease (or, you can write about it).

6. Draw the benefits (or, you can make a list of why this is so meaningful).

7. The next time you need to do this aspect of your work, schedule a few minutes of quiet time beforehand so that you can repeat this activity. Then complete the task at hand.

8. Make sure you plan some quiet time immediately afterwards, so you can regroup and recharge.

Pete, one of my introverted clients, would struggle in his own way. His mind would chatter away about how this was all too hard, how unimportant he was, how he would be better off just quitting. Before following up with a client, the chatter would start – had he done a good enough job, were they upset with him, had he really made a difference? Before signing off on a job, he would read and reread his work, the chatter asking the same sorts of questions – is this enough, is it right, do I need more quotes?

In our work together, we pinpointed the times when the chatter would start. I taught him this technique and he began using it straight away. Pete noticed that his confidence levels began to shift. When the chatter started up, Pete would take the reins and remind himself of how important his work is to the world – and then get out there and make a difference!

The key with this exercise is in recognizing the importance of your work – the meaning, value and gifts you bring to the world. When you do this, the significance of what you do very quickly outweighs your fears, mind chatter, and self-consciousness, your feelings of inadequacy, self-doubt and worry.

Trust in the importance of your work. You are the messenger. Deliver your message – with ease!

Tips for coaches
If you are a coach using this with your client, make sure you have a few large sheets of paper, some colored pencils, oil pastels and markers ready for this session.
Please understand that there are no judgments on artistic ability, this is entirely for your client… it is a powerful way to create shifts.

I have created a worksheet that you can use – you can find it here: http://bit.ly/IntrovertsPassion

This is a powerful way to connect in with the deeper meaning. For introverts, it is particularly empowering and can reignite passion and inspiration. It can also be used with extroverts who need a boost of confidence.

EXPECTATION RELEASE AND SURRENDER: HOW TO MANAGE YOUR EMOTIONS WHEN AWAITING AN IMPORTANT OUTCOME

By Kit and Rose Volcano

This exercise helps you surrender and release resistance when you want something badly and it's not coming. It's for anyone who is anxiously awaiting an outcome. When you are emotionally tied to getting the result you want, it means that your perceived worth, safety, or value is externally based. The shift your perception to being ok no matter what, you shift your value, safety, from that of an external focus to that of an internal focus.

Great for:

- People going through major life transitions: retirement, marriage, children, buying a house.
- People with anxiety or those that spend time worrying about whether things are going to work out the way they want.
- People who believe there is only one solution or pathway to their problem or one way to get what they want.

– – –

Have you ever caught yourself unable to feel calm and peaceful when you're anxiously awaiting an outcome, when you want something so bad that it hurts?

This might be you if you're checking your phone and your email constantly and feeling phantom vibrations in your pocket when you haven't received any new notifications. If you're unable to focus on anything else without having an answer or response about that:

- House
- Raise
- New job
- New love
- Safety of a loved one
- Pregnancy
- Business deal

This exercise will help you ease your mind and heart, and open the doors of creativity, hidden resources and potential you don't currently see because you're rigidly tied to a specific result. It also connects you to the energy of faith and the knowledge that everything will be ok.

When you're expecting a certain outcome, the brain is programmed, by nature, to look for any signs to confirm your worst fears or highest hopes, depending on where your mindset is. If your mindset tends to veer naturally into negativity, you will begin to find anything to confirm that the thing you dread the most will be happening soon and, after it does, life will be over.

The energy you bring to your personal interactions will reflect this as well. Your emails, calls and texts will come across desperate, needy and anxious, and you may end up sealing your own destiny with your vibration alone. When you can reprogram your habitual emotional patterns from fear to gratitude, not only will you feel better, but you'll attract more situations and interactions that match that positive energy you are putting out.

Steps

1. Brainstorm your other options
Make a list of every possible reason why everything is going to be great, even if the outcome is not what you expected or wanted. For example, we were anxiously awaiting a response from the landlord of the house we wanted. Our house was already packed and we were ready to move in an instant's notice. We made a list of every possible thing we could do with our time if we didn't get our desired outcome: take a national

park road trip in a rented RV, stay with friends or family that have been wanting a visit, or put our stuff in storage and house sit in Dallas for a family member.

2. Write a gratitude letter

Write a letter of gratitude to the person or the perceived thing that is holding up movement on the current situation. For example, I sat down and wrote a letter of gratitude to our future landlord, thanking him for choosing us as tenants, as though he already had. I even went out and bought him a bottle of wine and some delicious fresh baked cookies in expectation of a positive result.

3. Do something completely unrelated to the situation

Go for a walk, get a massage, get some frozen yogurt. Don't bring your phone. Let yourself completely detach from the outcome and focus on something else. For example, after we had made the list, and written the letter, I went grocery shopping and my partner went on a bike ride. By the time I had gotten home, the landlord had called and the place was ours.

By following these steps, you're rewiring your nervous system from panic mode to calm and confidence. When you rewire your automatic negative emotional patterns, you shift your entire vibration from one of scarcity to one of possibility. Not only does this process get you results in your life, but it allows you to feel better before the results come. Often times we desire results because of the way it will make us feel. Therefore, if you feel better first, you're already halfway there. This process has worked for us many times and we've seen amazing results with our clients as well.

Tips for coaches:

- When assigning this, you have to be unattached to the results your client will get from this coaching process. As a coach, when you detach from your client's results, it empowers them to be the master creator of their life (instead of their coach being the master creator).

Often when assigning this to a client it is good for you to do the assignment as well. Because our clients mirror us, if your client is coming to you with this specific issue, the same issue probably exists for you in a similar way. Are you still tying your worthiness, value, or safety to particular outcomes or results?

TURNING OBJECTIONS INTO SALES

By Dario Cuccio

This exercise helps those that have a business deal with customers to become more confident in handling objections and turning prospects into customers. It's for coaches, entrepreneurs and business owners that need to sell their services or products in order to be successful.

Great for:

- Life and business coaches that don't have much experience with sales.
- Business owners that find sales conversations challenging or uncomfortable.
- Entrepreneurs that want to improve their selling skills.

- - -

When you're looking for a sale, it's important that you ask for feedback during the entire sales process. This validates the customer and shows them that you are listening and genuinely concerned about their specific needs. Try to learn as much as possible about the customer during every single sales pitch.

It's normal to get some no's when you're having a sales conversation but it is also possible to turn those objections into sales. The first step is to relax. A customer will know if you tense up immediately after their objection. Next, listen and intently observe both the verbal and nonverbal messages the prospect is giving, what is being said and what is not being said. Question their objection to make sure that you both understand the initial reason why they don't want to make a purchase. That way, you are both on the same page and there is no misunderstanding when you attempt to smooth out their concern. Respond to the objection with genuine honesty, then confirm the customer's answer to your response before proceeding with the sales pitch.

You will know if you made the correct or incorrect response to their objection based on verbal and nonverbal cues that immediately follow your response. If your response was correct and on target, then the customer will become more engaged in the conversation. If not, they will persist with the same objection. At that point, you must backtrack to get more clarity on what the customer is really objecting to. Listen for unstated objections as well as the ones that the customer verbally communicates. Being sensitive to the specific needs and wants of each customer is the best way to form your response to any objection.

Objection resolution techniques
Another important part of turning objections into sales is to never let the customer view you as an obnoxiously persistent salesperson. Any good salesperson must learn how and when to resist, assist, and persist.

1. Resist
Resist the temptation to back off too early when faced with an objection. Hang in there. Also, resist the temptation to take the easy sale and not press on to fully solve the problem of the prospect.

2. Assist
Assist the customer in defining his or her real needs. Help him or her understand the basic problem that stimulated the objection. Don't just relate to the objection itself, but rather to the issue that really prompted the objection. Also, assist the person after the sale in gaining the maximum benefits from the product or service you have delivered. Follow up and follow through.

3. Persist
Persist in a way that shows that you genuinely want to be of service. When you use the techniques in the process we have described, you can persist without the intention of manipulating. You persist in a way that nonverbally conveys your concern and your sincerity. This strengthens the bond of trust between you and your potential customer.

Here are a few key techniques that will help you handle objections as they arise on the journey to converting a prospect into a customer:

1. Use "feel/felt/found"
Examples:

- "I understand how you feel" (I'm empathizing with you).
- "Many people have felt the same way (you are not alone in all this), however, they have found that . . ." (and you then present your solution).
- "I understand your thinking. I thought the same thing when I first saw this product. However, I have found that . . ."

2. Convert to a question
When the customer makes a statement, it can be difficult to keep the conversation moving but you can convert the statement into a question that allows you to answer more easily. Example: "I don't think I could use that product." Your response could be: "There is an important question I perceive in your statement and that is 'How can you gain maximum use from a product like this?'" Then proceed to answer the question, rather than rebut the statement.

3. Echo technique
Sometimes you are faced with a response from a customer that really doesn't give you enough information. In this case you can reflect or echo it back to the prospect. For example, the customer might say that the price is too high. Here, you can respond by saying, "Too high?" She or he will generally respond at that point by giving you more feedback and information. From there, you can address the concern about price from his or her perspective.

4. Lowest common denominator
In this case you take an objection which is a big issue in the customer's mind and reduce it to a smaller issue much easier to comprehend and handle. Example: "$300 is too much."

Response: "$300 does seem like a large price tag until you consider that you will probably be using this 3,000 times a year, which means that your cost per usage is only 10 cents; a small price to pay for the increased convenience and profitability that comes from this product."

As you proceed down the crossroads of communication on your way to sales success, you are bound to encounter many objections. Knowing how to handle them makes all the difference between a sale and losing a customer.

Action Items:
1. Now that you know more about your customer, ask them direct questions about the product. What needs to happen in order to satisfy your customer?

Implementation Tip: Come up with personalized solutions using your product in your customer's life. Example: "I bet these tickets would be a great gift for your wife. Didn't you mention your anniversary was coming up? I know a great baby sitter if you need one."

2. If a customer gives you an objection, do not get defensive. Instead, dig deeper.

Implementation Tip: Try asking them to specify what they are objecting to and the reason behind it.

3. After addressing the objection, always ask your customer to buy.

Implementation Tip: Try saying something like, "Are you ready to get started?" or "If I
do this for you, will you stay with our company as a satisfied customer?"

If you want more resources on how to sell effectively and turn prospects in customers, you'll find them here: https://dario-cucci-230a.mykajabi.com/pl/35202

START A MOVEMENT WITH YOUR MESSAGE: TURNING YOUR MESS INTO YOUR MESSAGE

By Erin Loman Jeck

Need to know how to craft a talk, tell your story, or create a message for your business, product, or service? With this exercise you will learn how to look at your life experiences and build a message that will create your own movement. It's for entrepreneurs that need a brand message, coaches who are speaking and selling, and career professionals who need to deliver presentations.

Great for:

- People who want to connect with their audience more deeply.
- Entrepreneurs and coaches who want to establish trust with potential clients or customers.
- Entrepreneurs and coaches who want to improve their public speaking.

- - -

Are you looking to create a compelling talk? Do you have a message you would like to create a movement around?

Today's culture is screaming for deeper connection, for vulnerability, for authenticity, for leaders who walk their talk, who are bold and brave enough to share their story with the world. We have all sat through speakers bragging about their successes and felt bored. But when we hear a speaker share their personal story of tragedy or overcoming adversity, we are mesmerized through the entire thing. What is it that captivates us?

Neuroscience is confirming that our nervous systems are wired for us to connect with other human beings. There have been studies that look at emotions such as disgust, shame and happiness, where the exact same areas of the brain light up in the person talking about their feelings and the listener. They believe that this is where empathy comes from – we listen to others and start to feel what they are experiencing. When we share our story, we are literally moving the audience to feel the same emotions.

If you're good at telling your story, the listener will look for a story in their own life that is similar to the story you're sharing. This is called commonality – when I see myself in you. It's important that you show your audience that you are them and they are you, because this builds trust and connection.

Recently, with the whole "me too" movement, something was brought to the surface that I have been speaking about for years – when you can share your story, you assist others in finding their own way through the experience. In my seminars, I give the participants "me too" signs, and anytime they hear a story that they connect with, they raise the sign to show the speaker that they are sharing a story that is resonating with them. This gives Instant feedback to the speaker so they know that their message is moving people and to keep going.

This exercise will help you craft stories from your life that you can use in your marketing, presentations, and speeches.

Exercise

Your biggest problems and your hardest days, when you looked around and had no answers, are your greatest stories. When we think about movies, we are always rooting for the underdog, not the bully. The audience wants to see that you have gone through some difficult stuff to get to where you are today.

Your mess is your message. The problems you have gone through and found solutions to are yours to teach people and help them transform their lives.

So how do you capture your story, you might be asking yourself? Let's jump in and discover the stories that you can start developing and sharing.

1. Write down a list of the top 10 worst things (rock bottom days) you have experienced.
Examples: I was 10 years old and my father died, at 15 my mom told me she was diagnosed with incurable cancer, I was cut from the volleyball team and told I should take up bowling, I was told by my math teacher I was a dumb blonde and wouldn't amount to anything. These are the pivotal moments that changed you.

2. Write down the lessons you learned through those tough days.
Did you increase your reliance, did you find a new super power, did you find a solution that has been proven to be a game changer, have you discovered something deeper about yourself? What are things you wish you could go back and tell yourself on those days? These are the lessons you can teach others.

3. Find out what you're an expert in.
There should be a couple of words that repeat in your lessons. What are the common themes? What are you an expert in based on these lessons?

Telling these stories can help you sell products, services, and even yourself. Use your own lessons to help others avoid your mistakes and offer the solutions you found to be effective. Use your stories to deeply connect with your audience, whether it's in a boardroom, from stage, or in a 1:1 conversation or coaching relationship – this is the key to deepening all of your relationships.

4. Tell your story to create a "me too" response.
Some of the most pivotal things to share that are universal in your story are:

- What was I thinking?
- What was I feeling?
- What was I experiencing in my physical body?

221

Illustrate what you were experiencing in that tough moment. For example, "I was so upset, I thought to myself 'who do you think you are'? I felt failure as if someone had sat on my chest and I couldn't breathe." These are things that everyone has experienced, even if it the specifics were different. Using these powerful descriptions really drives home the commonality we experience across sex, age, culture, religion, political parties, etc.

Case study
I had a client look at her list of bad days. She realized that she had never thought her mother's cancer diagnosis was an impactful moment that should be shared with others because it didn't seem to relate to her business. She examined what she had learned during that tough time – resilience, determination, the belief that anything is possible, and you are who you spend the most of your time with (her mother had cut people out of their lives who didn't support her "curing" her own illness). These lessons were super powerful for her to share with others in her business talks. As she was now able to deeply connect to her audience through this story, she began increasing the sales she brought in from speaking.

Tips for coaches
When sitting with your client, ask them to spend 3 minutes coming up with their worst day exercise. This gives them no time to overthink, they just have to write them down. Encourage them to get their thoughts out without editing, then they can start to go back and examine the lessons they learned from those seemingly "bad experiences". This is a powerful exercise for people to realize they are an expert in their own right and that others who are experiencing these situations can be served by them sharing their story.

YOUR VISION OF SUCCESS

By Richard Grillenbeck

This exercise helps you get clear about what motivates you, which values will carry you to success and what "success" really means for you. It's for individuals to use to get clear on their priorities or coaches to use with clients in one of their first sessions.

Great for:

- People who want clarity about their values
- People who want to define what success means for them.
- People who are struggling to achieve their goals but aren't sure why
- People starting to work with a coach but aren't sure what to focus on

— — —

If you ask someone what goals they want to reach or what success looks like for them personally you will get uncertain answers like "I do not know yet", "not sure" or vague answers like "a happy life". Without a clear vision of what motivates you and what success really means for you, it's not possible to know what type of actions you need to take to create success and happiness.

This exercise will help you to find out what you really want, what success means to you, what you want to strive for and what would motivate you on your way to your own vision of success. It will give you better insights of the values that will support you in reaching your own individual success, and will help you build a solid base for any personal growth that's needed on your path to success.

In this exercise we will use mind mapping to clarify your values and define your vision of success. Mind mapping is a simple technique for drawing information, instead of writing it in sentences. The drawings always take the same basic format of a tree, with a single starting point in the middle (a word or a question) that branches out into new points (words or phrases), and keeps dividing again and again.

I have found when working with coaching clients that mind mapping really helps visualizing their thoughts and feelings. Mind maps combine your logical and emotional ways of thinking and therefore help tremendously to get a complete picture of your topic/challenge onto paper.

Steps

In this exercise we use a traditional mind mapping technique but we also ask questions to access different parts of ourselves, including our "elder and wise soul" and our "inner child" so we can discover our deeper motivations and values.

1. Prepare one piece of paper (A3 or bigger) and a minimum of 5 pens (flipchart markers) with different colors.

Take one marker and draw a mind map with the central question: "What does success mean to me?" Draw 8-10 main branches answering with only one word on each branch. We will now perform a little mental exercise where creativity and imagination will help you to get some further insights.

2. Take another color. Imagine you meet a curious 75-year old former CEO of a company and you chat a little bit about success and what you think of it. What would you tell him? Which words would you choose? What comes up during the conversation? What topics are important for you? What would you not miss to tell this old-timer? What needs to be emphasized?"

Write these answers down on a separate piece of paper, one question at a time. This helps you connect with your inner "elder and wise soul". It also gets you into a mood to "think back from the end" instead of getting stuck because in your current situation you may not even see a way to success.

After you've finished, what would you like to add (using the 2nd color) to your mind map as a main branch or sub-branch?"

3. Take your 3rd color. Now imagine you're telling a very inquisitive 10 year old girl about what success means. Which key aspects do you focus on now? Which words are you using when telling her what success means for you? Which phrasing and wording is important?

This inner conversation helps you connect to your "inner child", to see things in a simplified way and to get fresh ideas. Add the new key points to your mind map.

4. Take a 4th color. Now imagine you are going to a conference and giving a keynote speech with the title, *What is success?* You are prepared, having taken your mind map with you, and feel very attuned to your expected audience. The organizer tells you that instead of 20, now 200 participants will listen. The crowd seems to be very curious and interested. The lightning is very pleasant, the acoustics are excellent and you make yourself comfortable on a bar stool. After a sip of water you start giving your speech. Now let yourself surprise yourself by what you are focusing on during the talk. Which aspects of success are important? What is your main statement?

This visualization takes you into an "inside-out state" where you can reflect on the topic as if you had to summarize and present it to an external audience. You may be surprised by what you imagine yourself saying. Add any new insights that come up in your visualized talk.

5. Now highlight five terms on your mind map which are the most important ones, using another color. You should now write these down as a list so that you can build sentences or short statements about what success means to you. Come up with five sentences which describe your conclusions about

225

success. You can use these sentences as a kind of affirmation to read on a daily basis. You may even condense them into one main statement.

Tips for coaches

- Allow enough time as this exercise usually takes a whole coaching session (approx. 45 min).
- You can help the client to get into a relaxed but focused mood using some background classical or instrumental music if you are in a live coaching session.
- In standard mind mapping different colors are used to address different topics or to emphasize main and sub-branches. In this exercise we use the colors to distinguish between different perspectives on "success" so make sure that you switch colors on each exercise step.
- You can also use this exercise for other topics like values, a certain belief, a resource, their partner, their job and so on.
- If you guide your client to create a new version of their mind map after a few months of coaching you can compare these two maps so they can understand their progress and evaluate the changes they have already implemented in their life.

CONFIDENCE FROM WITHIN: FIND AUTHENTIC CONFIDENCE IN UNCERTAIN SITUATIONS

By Jennifer Davoust

This exercise helps those struggling with perfectionism and procrastination get unstuck and begin moving towards new and uncertain territory with confidence. It's for people who experience lack of confidence, procrastination, and/ or perfectionism as a block to committed action. Mindset or business coaches will also find this exercise useful for their clients who suffer with these issues.

Great for:

- People who experience self-doubt, procrastination or self-sabotage and don't follow through on projects or goals.
- People who struggle with perfectionism and have trouble finishing tasks or feeling good about themselves.
- People who want more confidence to take on new tasks, activities or projects.

– – –

Confidence is a super power. When you are feeling confident you are more likely to take action, to jump on opportunities, and to demonstrate the tenacity and persistence it takes to reach success. You are also more likely to learn from your mistakes rather than take them personally.

However, we don't always feel confident stepping into the unknown. Our minds are wired to avoid the unknown and to seek out the familiar. Self-confidence can be defined as trust in one's ability to do something well. When you have done something many times you naturally build confidence in your ability. So how do you have confidence in yourself when the task at hand is new and unfamiliar? In this exercise we will

227

learn how to create confidence from the inside-out rather than the outside-in so that you can take on those new exciting tasks with a sense of certainty and trust in yourself.

As you approach the unfamiliar, your mind has a few strategies to keep you safely in the scope of what you already know. Self-doubt is the first thing most of us experience when stepping towards an unfamiliar goal. We all feel self-doubt in some form or another but it is not always obvious to us.

Doubt can manifest as procrastination, perfectionism and self-sabotage. Procrastination is that strong inclination to do anything other than the unfamiliar task. Perfectionism is the inclination to keep working on the task indefinitely so that the uncertainty of what others will think of your work is never met.

Self-sabotage can be the sneakiest of tactics your mind uses to keep you in the familiar and known. Self-sabotage generally sneaks in when you have overcome the first two strategies and put yourself out there in a new way. Your mind then gets to work manufacturing circumstances for you to feel the same rejection and disapproval that is so much safer and more familiar than any new found success.

As long as you rely on your previous experiences to feel confidence and banish doubt, the new and unfamiliar will always remain just out of reach. This exercise is designed to cultivate inner confidence in the qualities you bring into any situation, thereby curbing the self-doubt that comes with uncertainty. With renewed confidence you can once again turn your attention to making your dreams a reality.

The idea behind this exercise is simple. You already have all of the resources you need to succeed within you. How you utilize and appreciate these resources will determine your level of effectiveness in reaching your goals. This exercise is designed to bring your attention to the experiences and qualities you already have that can set you up for success in the future. Remembering that you have demonstrated tenacity, courage, flexibility, and intelligent problem solving in the past will support you in feeling confident you can do it again, even with the tasks ahead that are new and unfamiliar.

Steps

1. Describe the most successful version of yourself. What are the personality attributes, qualities, and skills you would need to be this version? (Focus especially on the qualities. E.g. courage, integrity, presence, leadership, outgoing, organized, consistent)

2. Identify the main quality you are looking to cultivate in your present situation. What would you need to demonstrate to guarantee your success in this new venture?

3. Identify a time in your life when you were powerfully exhibiting that quality. It could be when you were 5 years old on the playground and you exhibited leadership by spearheading a game of tag with your friends. Try not to judge the experience. Have yourself re-experience yourself in this memory. How did it feel? What happened? How did you see yourself?

   Know that this quality is within you and available at any time. If you demonstrated it before you can do it again.

4. Ask yourself why it is important for you to step into this quality in your present situation. What happens if you do? What happens if you don't?

5. Commit to taking action in your present situation from a place of confidence, just like you did in the memory you identified.

6. Remind yourself that you already have the capacity inside of you to get the job done. The most powerful thing we can have confidence in is our ability to figure things out.

229

Tips for coaches

The exercise is designed to shift focus from "confidence in what you know" to "confidence in who you are".

The exercise is comprised of four main parts;

1. The lack or what's missing in the situation
2. The focus or the qualities you need to bring
3. The vision or why it is important for you to succeed
4. The action and commitment to moving forward

Clients with a strong desire to have everything figured out before moving forward may be especially resistant. In that case I recommend spending extra time in step 4 and asking the question "What happens if I don't", where you can identify the pain of remaining stuck in perfectionism and procrastination. The key to this exercise is in trusting and knowing that everything your client needs to succeed and figure it out along the way is already within them.

Author Directory

Alessandra Patti

Qualifications/Services: Accredited Practitioner Coach for Assertiveness, Art Of Say No Coaching
Location: Zurich, Switzerland
Website: www.findyourway.company

Alessandra Patti, originally from Italy, resides in Zurich, Switzerland, where she founded her Coaching company, *FindYourWay*. She is an accredited practitioner coach, with a huge passion for writing since childhood, she enjoys reading and spreading her ideas around! She also has a master degree in Translation and Interpreting, a bachelor degree in Marketing and Branding, a Certificate of Analytical Psychology and, of course, Coaching.

Her company supports individuals and firms in being more assertive and self- confident by using language transformation techniques to become more diplomatic (how to say NO without actually pronouncing the word "No" is her favorite technique, as you can see in the book chapter). The results of her coaching are freedom,

233

a stop to guilt feelings, more happiness and better time management and boundaries for people.

Alessandra organizes workshops and coaching programs to reach assertiveness and speak one's mind. She also develops body language techniques to bring more confidence at the workplace and being able to ask virtually anything.

Alessandra teaches Cuban Salsa Dancing part-time (yes! Dancing is one of her passions too!) and developed a program that bridges Salsa and Coaching, called "Dance for Confidence", that gives people the courage to step outside their comfort zone and dance!

In her free time Alessandra enjoys salsa dancing in Zurich, reading, writing and spending time with her partner and their good friends just doing "those simple things that make one happy".

Aoife Gaffney

Qualifications/Services: Money coaching, money mindset mentor, one to one, group and online,professional speaker
Website: http://prudencemoneypenny.com/

Prudence Moneypenny Coaching is the brand name for Aoife Gaffney, money mindset mentor. She empowers women to take control of their financial freedom in a lighthearted and compassionate way.

Brendan Burns

Qualification/Services: Life & Business Coach and Influencer
Location: New York City
Website: www.brendanhburns.com

Brendan Burns is a Life & Business Coach delivering breakthroughs in any area of life. He has coached thousands of people through live & online programs to increase happiness, fulfillment & vitality.

Cassandra Galbier

Qualifications/Services: Licensed Massage Therapist, Body Memory Recall Practitioner, Yoga Teacher, Reiki Master offering private sessions and virtual group sessions
Location: Nevada City, CA
Website: www.actualizedaffinity.com

Cassandra is a graduate of the 675-hour Massage Program at Asheville School of Massage and Yoga (2012) and the 200 Hour YTT with Yogacara Global Teacher Training (2014). She became certified in Body Memory Recall (2012) with Jonathan Tripodi, and continued her bodywork studies in Cranial Sacral (2014), Thai Massage (2016), and studied Lomi Lomi in Hawaii with Kevin Kishida in 2018. She has worked in North Carolina, Costa Rica, Pennsylvania, and California. She is the visionary and former owner of A New Day: Massage & Yoga Studio, LLC in Warren, PA. Cassandra now works with her partner and Transformational Life Coach Leo Castrence at Actualize(d) Affinity offering packages, workshops, and retreats which guide individuals and parents towards tools of self-care, inner awareness, and living an authentic, abundant life.

Cassandra balances life between Nevada City, California with her son and partner, and traveling the world being inspired and inspiring others to live a passionate life walking one's unique path. Cassandra uses her trained hands and intuition to guide her to help each client with their specific needs. Combining Deep Tissue, Myofascial Release, Cranial Sacral, Body Memory Recall, Thai, and Lomi Lomi she is able to find the perfect balance of what will help you walk away feeling ReConnected and ReNewed. If you have any physical or emotional symptoms, and would like help supporting your body to unwind and work towards a more Vibrant Alignment, check out Cassandra's private sessions. She also has a virtual Creating Daily Ritual program you can join from anywhere in the world!

As new parents Cassandra and her partner Leo offer new online Parenthood Programs, available to help transform families and the paradigm of balanced parenting. Check out their website for current offerings.

Cecilia Olsson

Qualifications/Services: Chartered Physiotherapist with a Bachelor Degree in Behavioral Science
Location: Sweden
Website: www.lifepractice.se

Life will inevitably bring you in contact with pain and suffering, usually the only thing that differs between humans are how many birthdays you get to celebrate before you're faced with some serious difficulties. Pain and suffering are a natural part of life. Whatever situation you're facing though, you can always find ways to fill your life with meaning and vitality. Cecilia would know, as she's survived being severely ill with encephalitis and had to find her way back to a whole new way of living, using all her knowledge as a Physiotherapist within the Behavioral Field. Since 2008 Cecilia has been helping others move through fear, pain & difficulties to living meaningful and vital life's true to their values whatever life situation they've found themselves in. For a long time, the myth that feeling good means living a good life has made people lose track whilst chasing happiness instead of building a life of meaning and deepfelt vitality that they feel proud of.

Cecilia runs workshops for businesses, healthcare professionals, students and the general public on ACT with behavioral change, she is an authentic and appreciated public speaker. She invites her audience to learn through experience and whether it's health care professionals or the general public attending, her way of connecting through shared experiences, laughter and pain brings us together in our shared human fate – with our racing minds and our tendency to avoid uncomfortable emotions.

Do you want to learn how to move through difficulties and find pleasure and meaning right where you are? Visit our webpage, follow us on Instagram, Facebook or join our online training or contact us on info@lifepractice.se. We're looking forward to connecting with you and helping you find the tools that will bring you closer to the life you're longing for!

Chase Boehringer

Qualifications/Services: Founder of The Bucketlist Lifestyle
Location: San Diego, CA
Website: www.thebucketlistlifestyle.com

Chase Boehringer is from a tiny town in the Oregon wood. At 22 years old he found himself divorced, depressed and suicidal. After taking the long way to fulfillment and forgiveness for himself and others, he started The Bucketlist Lifestyle. Where he helps people live the life of their dreams, one Bucketlist item at a time. Chase is a Certified life coach and has used his coaching to transform lives all over the world. Chase spends most of his time leading small group adventures around the globe and connecting with people from all walks of life.

Christine Compas

Qualifications/Services: Intuitive Astrologer and Life Success Coach
Location: St. Louis, MO, USA
Website: www.christinecompas.com

Christine is a life success coach who utilizes astrology, intuitive insight, and other personal growth tools in order to help her clients gain clarity and focus around the steps they need to take in order to find their soul's true purpose and path in life. She is located in St. Louis, MO., but has worked with clients all over the world. Please check out her website to learn more about her offerings and services.

Claire Costello

Qualifications/Services: Intuitive Empowerment Coach
Location: World-wide
Website: cleartransmissions.com

Claire dances her unique rhythm around the world, providing Clear Transmissions to 1-1s, groups, workshops, retreats and festivals. She passionately guides and inspires those ready to "Embody, Express & Shine our Soul", live authentically free, healthy and empowered, creating and co-creating their destined ideal reality.

Claire is the Coach, Teacher & Energy Worker for you if you are looking for clarity, purpose, health, connection and alignment. Clear Transmissions is a deep life changing process for you to feel: clear on your life path, peace in mind, healthy in your physical body, reconnected with yourself, spirit and relationships, access deeper levels of intuition, self-healing and personal gifts, and be in-tune with your true essence.

Cynthia Moffatt

Qualifications/Services: Executive Coach & Consultant Offered
Location: USA and Canada
Connect: linkedin.com/in/cynthiamoffatt or cindy@cynthiamoffatt.com

Cynthia believes the success and sustainability of a family, community or organization is directly related to the effectiveness of its leaders. Her interest and expertise as Coach and Consultant lie in helping formal and informal leaders with the "doing" and "being" of leadership by balancing their achievement and relationship competencies.

Cynthia is certified through the Coaches Training Institute, whose prestigious CPCC designation is the most rigorous and respected in the industry. Trained in CTI's Co-Active Model®, her philosophy holds clients as naturally resourceful and whole and her approach is to elicit the skills and creativity people already possess. Using an array of proprietary tools and resources, her methodology guides clients first in the development of self-leadership skills before honing the skills required to lead others. In this way, she partners with clients to identify their unique, "context-free" leadership style paving the way for contribution that is both meaningful to them and impactful to the environment they serve.

Cynthia is a member of ForbesTM Coaches Council, an invitation-only community for world-class business professionals lending her perspective to the ForbesTM platform alongside other notable industry influencers. She has been credentialed by and is a longstanding member of the International Coach Federation, the global association of professional business and personal coaches, serving on its Chapter Board of Directors as President and as Director at Large.

A highly intuitive strategic thinker and centered communicator, Cynthia's ability to deeply connect and create powerful partnerships has her recognized as a natural leader in service to others

Daniel Brisbon

Qualifications/Services: Nature Connected Life Coach
Location: Denver, CO
Website: www.abovetreelinecoaching.com
Social Media: @abovetreelinecoaching

Daniel is a certified nature-connected coach in the greater Denver area. With a focus on personal transformation and an inside out approach to personal growth and change, he utilizes the great outdoors as a container for greater awareness and understanding of our own internal wilderness. Nature has served as a place of healing and growth in Daniel's personal life and he is passionate about sharing that same experience with his clients and students.

When Daniel is not working with clients in his personal practice, you can find him on his mountain bike exploring all the beauty and adventure that the Rocky Mountains in Colorado have to offer. He is a professional mountain bike racer and loves to integrate his work in personal development to his bike racing. And vice versa.

Daniel is also a mentor and coach for students going through the same nature-connected coaching program that he graduated from in Boulder, Colorado. The school is called the Earth Based Institute and it focuses on training and guiding students to becoming nature-connected life coaches.

Danielle Sangita

Qualifications/Services: Registered Yoga Teacher, Massage Therapist, Ayurvedic Practitioner
Location: Asheville/Black Mountain North Carolina
Contact: daniellerottenberg@gmail.com

Danielle Sangita Rottenberg is an Ayurvedic Practitioner, massage therapist, an Ayurvedic yoga therapist and Yoga teacher. At the age of 25, she started her own non-profit agency where she brought together the healing powers of the arts to people with developmental, physical, and emotional challenges. This non- profit, Creative Clay Cultural Arts Center, continues to this day, 23 years later and has been recognized on an international level for its success in integrating the arts with people of various challenges.

Danielle Sangita received her initial training in Ayurveda at the California College of Ayurveda in 2008. She furthered her studies in Ayurveda under the guidance of Dr. Paul Dugliss of New World Ayurveda, Dr. Light Miller of Ayurvedic College for Wellbeing and David Crow for

Ayurvedic Aromatherapy. She has extensive training in traditional ayurvedic therapies and modalities including abhyanga, shirodhara, marma therapy, aromatherapy, and herbal medicine to help those restore and rejuvenate. She has worked as a Pancha Karma Therapist at Blue Lotus Ayurveda in Asheville, with Vishnu Das, and The Art of Living/Shankara Ayurvedic Spa in Boone, receiving further education on the therapies involved with Pancha Karma treatments. As a massage therapist and yoga teacher, she integrates a wealth of healing knowledge and clinical experience into her Ayurveda consultations, classes, and workshops. She currently maintains a successful and growing private practice in Black Mountain and Swannanoa for the last decade. In 2015, Danielle founded her second non-profit organization: The Yoga Service Movement, where she provides free yoga and health/wellness classes to underserved populations. This has continued to grow in popularity as the need is great. She continues to grow as a practitioner and is currently pursuing her interest in energetic healing, reiki and Chakra balancing and would like to expand into working with women in the Profit and Nonprofit Sector.

Dario Cucci

Qualification/Services: International Keynote Speaker, Bestselling Author & Serve And Sales Coach
Location: Switzerland & London
Website: www.dariocucci.com

Brings along over 20 years of Experience. He has developed his own Sales Communication Program that teaches Business Owners on how to increase Sales whilst retaining their existing Customers happy.

Derek Loudermilk

Qualifications/Services: High Performance Business Coach, Founder of AdventureQuest and the Art of Adventure, Author of Superconductors: Revolutionize Your Career and Make Big Things Happen
Location: St. Louis, Missouri/Global
Website: derekloudermilk.com
Social Media: @derekloudermilk

Derek has helped hundreds of entrepreneurs, adventurers, and thought leaders launch and grow their businesses through his coaching programs, AdventureQuest trips, the Art of Adventure Podcast, International speaking appearances, and his books, including Superconductors: Revolutionize Your Career and Make Big Things Happen.

Derek's mission is to help you feel like the most interesting person in the world, and believes that Adventure, Entrepreneurship, and Self-Actualization are key endeavors to that end.

After losing his house to a flood, nearly dying from a blood clot in his brain, a divorce, and dropping out of grad school, Derek re-started his career with a clean slate and vowed to make it the most daring adventure possible.

His life and work centers around values like being outside, asking better questions, lifelong learning, seeking the magic in everyday situations, dreaming and playing bigger, experimentation, communing remarkable people, and strategic thinking.

Diane Hopkins

Qualifications/Services: Book Coach, Content Coach (Courses & Presentations), Editor
Location: Bali-Australia-Europe
Website: wordandwing.co
Social Media: @wordandwing or facebook.com/wordandwing

Diane Hopkins helps coaches and entrepreneurs find their most powerful message so they can reach larger audiences and make a bigger impact on the world. She coaches people to write engaging books, create transformative online courses and prepare life-changing presentations and keynotes that connect with their audience and inspire real change.

With her background as a university teacher, author and speaker, Diane guides future thought leaders to create inspiring content that draws on their best strengths and connects with their ideal audience. She believes in the transformative power of teaching what you know and combining your unique combination of skills and life experiences to truly enjoy your work and live out your purpose.

Diane will help you find your unique writing, teaching and presenting "voice" and show you how to deliver your message with more clarity and confidence. She offers 1:1 coaching, runs live online group training courses and hosts writing retreats in Bali.

Diane has helped coaches and entrepreneurs: write books; create online courses, masterminds and group coaching programs; plan the content for their retreats; and prepare for keynote and conference presentations. She is committed to supporting tomorrow's thought leaders in finding the clarity and confidence they need to fulfill their dreams of inspiring bigger audiences.

Donita Brown

Qualifications/Services: Working Mom's Productivity Coach and Speaker
Location: Nashville, TN
Website: www.donitabrown.com

Donita is a listener and encourager for working moms. She helps working moms set up systems to help them accomplish what matters most.

Erik Hamre

Qualifications/Services: Skill Development Designer
Location: Worldwide
Website: the100hourchallenge.com
Connect: Erik Hamre(fb) erik.hamre@gmail.com

Studied skill development for last 5 years. Travelled to 70+ countries. Former professional poker player. Learner of all type of skills.

Erika Fitzgibbon

Qualifications/Services: Career, Business, Life Coach and Counselor
Location: St. Louis, Missouri
Connect: https://www.facebook.com/ EmpoweredImageCoaching
Social Media:@empoweredimage

Erika Fitzgibbon has more than 20 years experience in career counseling and coaching with diverse populations of clients including students, new and seasoned professionals, business owners and job seekers. She is a classically trained psychotherapist at the masters level and uses a powerful combination of coaching techniques as well as career and personal counseling methods. Her work is informed by multiple theories including career development, cognitive behavioral, asset based, family systems and more. In addition to her coaching work, Erika is an accomplished, award winning photographer who grew her business over 7 years time, until she retired to focus on coaching others to realize their dreams. Erika uses various counseling modalities, coaching exercises, story-telling techniques and design thinking concepts to empower people, help them identify their true calling, grow business, seek new opportunities and create one of kind, healthy, values drive professional and personal lives.

Erin Loman Jeck

Qualifications/Services: Executive and TEDX Speaking Coach
Location: Seattle, WA
Website: www.erinlomanjeck.com
Social media: @erinlomanjeck, https://facebook.com/erinlomanjeck

CEO of Transformational Speakers Agency, Executive Speaking Coach, TEDx Speaking Coach, and the Creator of Speakers Success Summit.

This highly sought after business coach transitioned to opening her own Speakers Agency. She is the leading authority on assisting thriving purpose-driven entrepreneurs in how to monetize their message, make an impact, influence change, and inspire action in others.

Erin's approach to speaking is unique and powerful, she utilizes the Psychology of Connection to illustrate how you can unlock any audience's trust and rapport, which leaves them feeling better about themselves and challenged to adopt your new idea or perspective. Leaders seek her out to learn how to be more powerful in their influence, especially in the C-Suite of organizations. If you are looking for a proven professional who is an impactful and influential trainer to lead your team or organization, or for executives to learn her techniques, then look no further. Erin's clients rave about the powerful impact she has made on them and her ability to help them find the subtle nuances that can take your influence and speaking to the next level.

Helene Weiss

Qualification/ Services: NLP Master Practitioner & Life Coach
Location: United Kingdom
Website: www.heleneweisscoaching.com
Social Media: @heleneweisscoaching

Helene is an NLP Master Practitioner & Life Coach. German by nationality and a former humanitarian worker with a Masters Degree in Diplomacy, she's served in various countries around the world before making a transition to setting up her own coaching business from Bali. Today she facilitates her clients' journey from feeling stuck to taking action in changing careers and living a meaningful life on one's own terms. True to her freedom spirit, she works with clients online and facilitates workshops both in Bali and England, her home bases of choice.

Ian Griffith

Qualifications/Services: Speaker, Coach, Author, Leader
Location: San Francisco, California
Website:www.facebook.com/iancgriffith
Social Media: @iancgriffith

Hi! I'm Ian Griffith. I'm a certified Coach, Speaker, and Leader with an expertise on mindset and what it takes to overcome fear and manifest our greatest dreams.

I am the founder of "Mindset Programs" which specializes in delivering extraordinary results to hundreds of members through online masterminds, top-tier speakers and transformative coaching. I am an expert in adding value to my tribe and giving them the power to transform their lives with outstanding results.

I am the leader of 14,500+ people in the world's largest Tony Robbins Fan Facebook group. I have led groups of people to feed and coach the homeless every week for a year. I know the power of contribution, of gratitude and I know the secret to living is giving.

I went to Tony Robbins 2 years ago, and he made me realize I had bargained away my dreams until they had been almost forgotten. I vowed never to let that happen again, to say "Yes" to life, no matter what. Since then I have coached hundreds of people around the world, and I have spoken in front of thousands of people live. I have been honored to be mentored, coached and taught by many of the best minds in the world.

Recently, I've been speaking with Joseph McClendon III and have had the opportunity to wake up hundreds of people to overcome their "Soulcrastination."

Soulcrastination defined as – "The putting off or delaying our soul's purpose"

The purpose of my life is to impact the world for good in a massive way. Here is nothing I like more than to help people breakthrough to their greatest version of who they are meant to be.

Dr. Jennifer B. Rhodes

Qualifications/Services: Licensed psychologist, relationship expert, and coach for creative professionals
Location: New York, NY
Website: www.visualartsreimagined.com and www.RapportRelationships.com

Dr. Jennifer B. Rhodes is a licensed psychologist, relationship expert, and consultant to creative professionals all over the world. She provides therapeutic, consultation, and coaching services to creative professionals worldwide. She is the founder of Rapport Relationships and Visual Arts Reimagined, as well as the forthcoming author of Relationships Matter Most.

Jennifer Davoust

Qualifications/ Services: Self Love Coach
Location: Columbus, Ohio
Website: www.jenniferdavoust.com
Social Media: @jenniferdavoust

Jennifer Davoust is a spiritual teacher and self love coach who knows how essential this love is to every success we crave. Jennifer is the host of the Tune Into You meditation podcast and creator of the Embodied Empath workshop in Columbus Ohio. Through her programs, Jennifer creates massive shifts in the way her clients see themselves and therefore the world. Her Embodied Empath workshops support the sensitive souls of the world in setting healthy boundaries and finding the gift in their ability to connect deeply. Certified by the Facilitator In Transformation program with Chris Lee and a graduate of the most prestigious hypnotherapy school in the world with a concentration in neuro-linguistic programming, she has impacted hundreds of people with her coaching and mentoring. Jennifer is a truth seeker and has been studying the self and our relationship to the subconscious mind since childhood. From struggling with depression and failed attempts at suicide to now teaching confidence on a daily basis, Jennifer is interested in how we can rewrite the scripts we follow in our minds. Jennifer will listen deeply, meet you where you're at, and walk with you to that next place you want to go. Jennifer has a compelling story and a unique perspective to offer when it comes to changing our minds about who we are and what we are capable of. When Jennifer is not busy spreading her message of self love you can find her exploring her local parks and connecting with nature. To connect with what Jennifer is up to be sure to find Jennifer Davoust on social media.

Joey Romeu

Qualifications/Services: Master Trainer from the European Institute of Fitness
Location: UK
Website: https://p2pfitness.co.uk/

My passion for all aspects of health, fitness, and sports psychology means I'm delighted to be able to make a living helping other people become happier with themselves, and supporting them in overcoming whatever mental or physical limitations they feel are stopping them from getting results.

As well as having graduated as a Master Personal Trainer and Nutrition Coach, I'm also a Certified Exercise Specialist, qualified Fat Loss Specialist, and I've worked for Disability Challengers – where I encouraged teenagers with special needs to get involved with sports and fitness.

In 2015 I worked for David Lloyd Leisure as a personal trainer and held weekly healthy eating seminars with a holistic approach to nutrition and lifestyle management. I now work as an independent mobile personal trainer, and online Nutrition & Transformation coach.

In 2016 I qualified as a DNAFit coach so that I could help people achieve their health, fitness, performance or weight loss goals by personalising their fitness and nutrition based on their genetics.

I also certified as a Master Coach under Tony Robbins trained Master Coaches Tony and Nicki Vee so that I could become a world class coach and help people with not just their health and fitness, but also any other challenges people face that hold them back from being their best self and living an extraordinary life.

Julia Melnova

Qualifications/Services: Lifestyle enhancement coach
Location: Florida
Contact: www.themagnificentduo.com

Julia Melnova is a lifestyle enhancement coach that has traveled the world seeking the top trainers in each technique she has mastered including Neurolinguistic Programming, Ho'oponopono and Reiki, and has used this knowledge to craft a unique approach that has helped clients worldwide to achieve the dual goal of success and happiness.

Her signature program, the Magnificent Duo, breaks down the myth that love must follow success and illustrates and explains how finding your perfect partner can in fact help you to improve your personal life and your career exponentially and how having a baby can bring priorities and values into focus.

Julia is also the mastermind behind AMZ Visionary Consulting, a marketing consulting agency that serves clients in the US and the UK. Through AMZ Visionary, Julia leverages years of experience in the e-commerce industry to guide e-commerce businesses in the optimization of their selling and operating strategy.

Julia's accolades include two Masters' degrees, in Business and in Law Administration, achieved with distinction at respected universities. She moved from Russia to Manhattan when she was 19 years old to pursue her dreams and has remained committed to make them a reality via continuous self development.

Kathy Hammonds

Qualifications/Services: Holistic Health Coach
Location: Rootstown, Ohio, United States
Website: kathammonds.com
Social media: @coachkathammonds

Kathy helps middle-aged folks break through their struggles with weight and chronic conditions. With over 30 years of experience in the healing arts, Kathy gently bridges the gap between tried and true ancient teachings and modern science. Her insightful, wise and caring teaching style has brought hundreds of individuals from a state of dis-ease back to their natural state of robust health.

Kathy offers her teachings as a way to approach health and healing with reverence and gratitude. Her classes, one-on-one sessions and workshops are a masterful, candid blend of attention, surrender, and delving deeply into one's body, mind and heart.

A devoted activist supporting personal freedom, simplicity and treading softly, you can often find her at her Ohio co-housing farm and retreat space, gardening, sprouting, preparing super-food meals, teaching Ayurvedic cooking, and coaching clients to unravel the source of their deep-seated pain. Clients get results that are profound and way beyond their expectations.

Keegan White

Qualifications/Services: Life and Mindset Coach
Location: Durham, North Carolina, United States
Website: www.keeganwhitecoaching.com

Keegan White is a Life and Mindset Coach, author, and speaker who support people to live their best lives by unlocking their highest potential. With over a decade of experience coaching people to break through habits, patterns and limiting beliefs, she has helped countless individuals live the life that they are destined to live.

Kelly Biasiolli

Qualifications/Services: Facilitator & Coach of Transformative Life Experiences & Adventures
Location: Appalachian Mountains and U.S. Desert Southwest
Website: www.meetthemomentwell.com

Seeking to learn from life's everyday adventures, Kelly strives to recognize the beauty and simplicity of each day, each moment. Her journey has led her to various countries all over the world, facilitating yoga teacher trainings, instructing backpacking, rock climbing and adventure courses, offering leadership development programs to corporate and collegiate groups, mentoring and training Outward Bound staff, and developing youth programs as a Peace Corps Volunteer.

Kelly is passionate about helping people step more fully into the present through a broad spectrum of adventure challenge activities, to stillness and observation of the body. She has extensive experience working with individuals and groups and takes a somatic (body-centered) approach to helping people become their best selves, inviting them to step into their authentic path.

With a BS degree from Texas A&M University, Kelly has completed over 1,000 hours of Yoga Teacher Training, is a Licensed Massage Therapist, and has completed the Rock Guide Course and Single Pitch Instructor Certification with the American Mountain Guides Association.

Kerry LiBrando

Qualifications/Services: Educational Consultant
Location: Washington D.C.
Contact: klibrando5688@gmail.com
Social Media: @kerplunk1012

Kerry is an educator at heart. She has always been inspired by the bravery of students and teachers. Classrooms, whether in schools or museums, are places where truly transformational conversations happen. Kerry's passion is to prepare and support educators in their quest to pursue justice for their students.

While currently serving in her seventh year as a classroom teacher, Kerry has also spent time as a museum education professional. She has spent time developing a deep knowledge and appreciation for the power of museums and historic sites while working as a National Park Service ranger, museum tour guide, and educational contractor.

Kerry is looking to support any leader or educator looking to understand their own identity better. Such knowledge is not only necessary, but is an incredibly powerful tool for changing the world and battling injustice.

In addition to teaching and coaching, Kerry spends her free time with her husband, Danny, and one-year-old daughter, Olivia. They spend their time, biking and checking out the museums in the D.C. area.

Kit & Rosie Volcano

Qualification/Services: Transformational Coaches
Location: San Diego CA
Website: thelittlevolcano.com

Kit & Rosie are a transformational coaching couple from San Diego. Their coaching programs empower healers and conscious entrepreneurs to embody their power to create businesses that thrive.

Laura Hardy

Qualifications/Services: Licensed Massage Therapist, Wellness Educator, and Homeopathic Consultant
Location: The Serenity Center Greenville, NC
Contact: www.laurahardywellness.com, ljhwellness@ icloud.com

Laura Hardy is a Homeopathic consultant, wellness educator, and a Licensed Massage Therapist. She became a licensed massage therapist in April of 2002 after studying at the Center for Massage and Natural Health in Asheville, NC. Over the years she has specialized in a variety of styles of massage and bodywork, including Reiki, Craniosacral, Lymphatic, Swedish, Deep Tissue, Pregnancy and Infant massage. She believes that Massage and Bodywork helps keep our bodies balanced so we can achieve the best state of Health and Wellness. In addition, she offers wellness education for individuals seeking clarity to the overwhelming and confusing world of health and wellness today.

In April of 2010 Laura studied and trained with Russell Mariani. Russell Mariani is a Health Educator, Nutrition Counselor and Digestive Wellness expert. He has been in private practice since 1980. He is the author of the book, Healing Digestive Illness, and the blog; The Roots of Health. In 2008 Laura studied Alternative medicine at Everglades University, where her love of homeopathy began. Since this time she has been learning everything she can about this amazing medicine. In 2014 she began studying with Joette Calabrese, leading study groups and helping her friends and family. In August of 2017 she began studying with Robin Murphy at the Lotus Health Institute, where she is in the process of receiving her certification of H.HOM and is working on her D.HOM. In Laura's holistic practice she encourages and instructs individuals with a progressive approach to healthy living. She assists them in finding clarity of health and wellness and guiding them to reaching their optimal state of balance. Wellness Education embodies the knowledge of food, homeopathy, diet, exercise and everyday well being.

Lee McKing

Qualifications/Services: Hypnotist
Location: Singapore
Website: www.leemcking.sg
Social Media: facebook.com/LeeMcKingTheHypnotist/

Lee McKing is a certified Basic and Master Practitioner of Neuro Linguistics Programming (NLP) as well as a certified Conversational Hypnotherapist and started his hypnotherapy practice in 2015. He has advanced his training to be a Certified Hypnosis Speaker and Presenter, and has given talks and workshops at schools and in public.

In 2016, McKing was interviewed and featured in The New Paper as well as 2 magazines, M Lifestyle and Vanilla Luxury. He was featured in various business and health blogs and interviewed by Yellow Pages in 2017. McKing is also one of the co-authors of "Because I'm Introvert, I Triumph" and "The Better Business Book".

In 2018, he was interviewed and featured in Style Guide, The Asian Entrepreneur and on Toggle, Singapore's online media platform. McKing first used hypnosis to heal from his post traumatic stress disorder (PTSD) and depression, and since then, begun his hypnosis practice in 2015.

He has used his skill and knowledge to help people solve specific problems in the areas of anxiety, anger, phobias and trauma. His expertise has helped his clients find the peace and freedom they have been searching for. He also helped people move forward in life, such as overcoming procrastination or finding forgiveness and letting go of the past.

McKing has also helped people with unique issues or even issues that most people do not usually think a hypnotist can help in, such as dyslexia, bulimia, and even in removing business blocks for success. McKing's unique approach to hypnotism has helped many people resolve their issues within a session. His curious mind allows him to explore the power of the mind. His friendly and open personality allows clients to share in an open and safe environment.

Leo Castrence

Qualifications/Services: Fatherhood Coach, Psychosynthesis Transformational Life Coach
Location: Nevada City, California
Website: www.actualizedaffinity.com
Contact: actualizedaffinity@gmail.com

Leo Castrence is a Passionate and Loving Father, Certified Psychosynthesis Transformational Life Coach (PLC), Fatherhood New Paradigm Hacker, Mens Work Facilitator, and a Relationship Alchemist.

Leo is a Psychosynthesis Life Coach (PLC), certified in 2018 with the 120-Hour Nationally Certified Psychosynthesis Coach Training Program through the Synthesis Center. As a Transformational Coach, he feels deeply called to create more resources and support for new and becoming Fathers. As a Father himself, he went through the lessons and obstacles in the new territory of Fatherhood. He eventually learned how much powerful resources and support existed for the Mommas and babies but was lacking for Fathers.

Leo then intentionally went into deep self-exploration and research with the support of his life partner Cassandra. In his experience, he found (and continues to explore) patterns and "struggles" that are common among fathers.

His mission is to help Fathers become the best version of themselves and create balance and harmony within families. His intention is to guide Fathers to be the best support possible for their partner, child, and Self while creating the Higher quality of life they desire for their family. He offers one-on-one and group sessions, helping to redefine the new Fatherhood Paradigm.

What would Life be like if you turned yourself all the way on?

Lisa Kniebe

Qualifications/Services: Content Coaching, Message Strategy and Communication Training
Location: Perth, Western Australia
Website: www.lisakniebe.com
Social media: @wordsthatshine

Lisa helps business owners share their message, get clear on what makes them unique and confidently become a leading voice in their industry. As a content and messaging coach for thought leaders, entrepreneurs and consultants, Lisa helps bring clarity to the content creation process.

Lisa has a knack for creating calm, helping clients sail past overwhelm into equilibrium. Originally a Neonatal Intensive Care Nurse, she's compassionate whilst being clear and decisive. Her coaching has moved many a stressed business woman from crisis to confidence.

But don't be fooled by Lisa's gentle demeanour, she is relentless in her pursuit of excellence. She's fearless when it comes to asking the tough questions that accelerate your growth. As a strong advocate of getting out of your comfort zone, Lisa walks her talk with frequent adventures, in her business and personal life (at 16 she sailed the North sea, at 46 she'll be climbing Mt Kilimanjaro).

Lisa has been in pursuit of self-knowledge since 12 years old, when her father gave her an astrological natal chart for Christmas. It was inscribed with the quote "Know Thyself". From that time onwards, she has been on a quest for personal development. This has contributed to her restlessness, as she's always been hungry for more than a conventional career could offer.

Lisa founded Stella Polaris Copywriting in 2016 and began her business journey. Highly talented, but without much business sense, she learned many lessons the hard way! Determined, resilient and in demand, her business grew. For three years Lisa worked in her zone of excellence as a writer, but now, as she launches Lisa Kniebe.com she moves into her zone of genius as a coach.

It's here she's helping the next generation of entrepreneurs create positive change in the lives of others with powerful communication.

Lois & Julia Thompson

Qualifications/Services: We are both Energy Practitioners, Certified Life Coaches, Infinite Possibilities Teacher Trainers, and Lois is also an Ordained Minister and Qi Gong teacher
Location: Erie Pennsylvania, United States
Website: www.quantumbalanceerie.com
Social Media: www.facebook.com/quantumbalanceerie

Lois and Julia Thompson are dedicated to assisting others heal themselves from the inside out through Positivity, Possibilities, and New Perspectives. Lois practices Pranic Healing and Julia is a Reiki Master Teacher. Both are certified Life Coaches. In an individual session with either Lois or Julia, they combine energy work, life tools, thought management and energy management techniques to provide unique assistance and results for their clients. Lois enjoys teaching Mike Dooley's Infinite Possibilities course and Qi Gong in the community. Julia finds it very fulfilling to teach her Reiki students and to offer unique Metaphysical classes in the community. She is also known locally for being a Crystal Goddess through teaching metaphysical classes on stones and through selling crystals.

Lucida Curran

Qualifications/Services: Introvert Empowerment Leader
Location: Australia
Website: www.LucindaCuan.com

I guide introverts to authetically shine in business in their unique way, without ehausting themselves to be seen and heard. I am passioate in supporting introverts to share their gifts and talent.

Mike Ratf

Qualifications/Services: Nution, Fitness and Team Building Coach
Location: Cincinnati Ohio
Contact: www.mikeratliffwellness.com,
mikeratliffwellness@yahoo.com

I am a Physical Education eacher by education. I am a personal trainer, nutrition, fitness and team building coach by life experience. Based on my interests, I have found a love for helping others find what gets them moving towards their goals. Whether it be a weight management goal, fitness goal or a business goal, I have something that will help. It has been said that everyone needs a coach and I am no exception. I am blessed by many mentors and coaches that help me get better every day. This allows me to pay it forward and help those around me. Through trial and error, some tears and a lot of hard work, I use a system that has stood the test of time and is proven to be effective.

Monica Devanand-Rajasagaram

Qualifications/Services: Life Coach
Location: Melbourne, Australia
Website: www.abouther.com.au

Monica is a wife, mother of two girls, a Medical Dr of 11 years, a published author and a Life Coach. She obtained her Life Coaching certification through Life Breakthrough Academy, which has helped her coach women through different phases of life. She coaches women to rediscover their identity, passion and purpose; to live a more fulfilling and authentic life.

Apart from coaching women, she also loves to inspire young girls through a global movement called GIRLIFE Empowerment. GIRLIFE Empowerment is a series of workshops for young girls, to inspire and equip young girls with life skills, to help them discover their innate strengths and power, and to inspire them to use these skills in their everyday life.

Monica is the first leader in Australia to run these life skills and empowerment workshops for young girls in Melbourne, Australia and wants to inspire as many girls as she can, to empower them towards living a healthier, happier and more peaceful life.

Monica is passionate about seeing women in meaningful community with one another, pursuing their calling and embracing life and all its challenges. She loves to bring women together, and is now also a leader of a global community of women, called Kingdom Women Entrepreneurs. Through this, she brings women together in an inspiring and relaxing environment to learn, feel empowered and form lifelong friendships.

Out of work, she enjoys time with her family and her children. She loves a good coffee, and spending time indulging in a good book! She loves the sun and Spring – when everything comes to life and blooms again.

Nik Wood

Qualifications/Services: Life Coach & Host of the Life Athletics podcast
Location: World wide
Website: lifeathletics.com

Nik Wood is a roving Canadian man who loves nothing more than experiencing and championing the greatness in others and in the world.

He is a coach and the host of the Life Athletics Podcast. His coaching life started when he became a certified NLP, Hypnotherapy, and Timeline Therapy practitioner at the age of 19.

Absolutely fascinated with what brought about greatness in others, Nik has put himself in positions to observe and learn from a wide variety of extraordinary people. From NBA athletes, top level tennis stars, Olympians, business people, artists, actors, musicians, humans, Nik has interviewed, observed, and learned from these people. He uses those learnings to help others to level up in their lives and to continually level up in his own.

Orian Marx

Qualifications/Services: Life Coach
Location: New York City, New York
Website: www.artoflifecrafting.comorian@
artoflifecrafting.com
Social Media: @orian (Twitter)

Orian is a life coach and creator of the Lifecrafting Framework for envisioning and realizing your best self. In addition to his coaching work, he has over a decade of experience as a user experience consultant and front end web developer delivering solutions for major corporations and state government agencies.

Orian serves as a Co-Chair of the Futurism Lab at NEXUS, a global non-profit dedicated to connecting young philanthropists with leading activists. He also volunteers with the Louis August Jonas Foundation which facilitates an international youth leadership summer program. His passions include travel, photography, swing dancing, emerging technology, and of course, personal development.

He resides in New York City (where he was born and raised) with his two favorite ladies - his wife Abril, and Olive, his cat.

Patricia Cimino

Qualifications/Service: Certified Life Coach
Location: Chicago Illinois
Website: www.patriciacimino.com

Patricia guides women "wantapreneurs" to become entrepreneurs. She helps them build a strong positive mindset so they can do what they're passionate about with clarity, confidence and optimism.

Paul Kuthe

Qualifications/Service: Business Coach
Location: Portland, Oregon
Website: Paul@tributarycoaching.com

Paul launched his career as a professional "action sports" coach and athlete developing and managing programs for a leading company in his field. It was during those adventures that he learned the importance of coaching, commitment, and operating in the moment with intense focus and determination while simultaneously managing fear and self-doubt. The natural world, like the business world, can be one of life's greatest teachers if you 'attend class' on a regular basis.

He's started kayaking some of the most demanding rivers anywhere at a young age. Soon after moving to Oregon he was making appearances in numerous film projects taking him to the very brink of what can be done in a sea kayak for National Geographic. Paul became a frequent a guest coach at the top international symposiums in the years to follow. Paul served as a Marine Technical

Advisor to Paramount Pictures and made appearances in national television ad campaigns for companies like Keen Footwear and Tampax. He even worked a day on the set of "Portlandia" personally coaching actor Fred Armisen and serving as an expert consultant. Despite the long list of accomplishments, Paul's most proud of his volunteer efforts spent cleaning his local rivers and fighting for access to clean water even gracing the pages of the NY Times in defense of free flowing rivers.

Paul launched Tributary Coaching LLC to bring his knowledge and coaching skills to the corporate world creating positive change in the lives of business professionals striving for the same sort of success and happiness. He and everyone here at Tributary Coaching LLC are driven to help people thrive while finding happiness and renewed purpose in their lives.

Paul is a TetraKey qualified Lead Trainer and Performance Coach with over two decades of coaching and training experience.

Rebecca Privilege

Qualification/Services: Family Freedom Coach, Health & Wellness Coach, Laughter Coach
Location: Secret Harbour, Western Australia and online
Website: www.rebeccaprivilege.com
Contact: rebecca@rebeccaprivilege.com

I help to restore your divine birthright to be healthy, happy and whole using my intuitive healing gifts combined with hypnotherapy, reiki and family freedom coaching.

It took a near death experience to find the courage to own my true calling. I'd been a NAET practitioner working in a Wellness centre in Fremantle, treating clients and getting amazing results. Little did I know that events would unfold that would shake my world. I'd stopped listening to my own body and didn't notice the sudden decline in my energy levels. In truth, I was ignoring the signals, the deeper issues. Ignoring continual nudges meant there was only one way to get my attention – a catastrophic physical, emotional and mental medical event; sudden onset acute microcytic anaemia.

After weeks of investigations I was finally getting somewhere and was seen by a leading specialist when I collapsed. The resus team were called and I was rushed to ICU, they discovered I had a Pulmonary embolism. After 6 days in ICU I was back on the ward and saw my friend, when she asked "So, Mate, want to check out do you?" it was a lightbulb moment. I realised had a choice. It was then I knew in my heart of hearts that I had been sent back for a reason – to live life on purpose, in healing and in service.

Today I am following that path with Rebecca Privilege Integrative wellness. It's here I eliminate physical and emotional pain, build self-belief and reconnect families in harmony and health. What do I believe? Where intention goes energy flows, we create our own reality. Dis-ease begins and ends with our emotions, which empowers all of us to take ownership and reverse this imbalance. All healing starts with you first, regardless of age.

Dr. Ing. Richard Grillenbeck

Qualifications/Services: Business-Coach Offered
Location: Metropolregion Nürnberg
Website: www.business-coach.de

Since more than 20 years I have been working in international teams as trainer, project manager, roll out manager and business coach. The pressure, deadlines, high expectations to deliver perfect results in almost no time and also intercultural fun – I had it all. And I strongly believe that one can take it if certain conditions are met. That is why I love to work as trainer and coach.

I speak German as my mother tongue and love to talk in English to people coming from many different countries.

As a coach I support you in changing: changing processes, ways of communication, methods of cooperation. To serve my German coaching clients I have written a book together with Jürgen Schimmel: "TEMP-Coaching" is available in German bookstores and online shops. Visit my blog to read more about it.

As certified trainer I assist you in international training rollouts bringing change and new processes into the teams.

As active member and chapter host of International Coach Federation I pledge to the code of ethics of ICF.

Rick Sharpe

Qualifications/Services: Life Coach, Emotional Intelligence and Mindfulness Facilitator
Location: Dubai, UAE
Website: www.rick-sharpe.com

After experiencing the deeper emotional trauma of personal heartbreak and trying to manage deeper bouts of depression, Rick made a life-changing decision to embark on a journey of healing through mindfully feeling. After "accidentally" writing a book about the experience, his goal is to promote mental health awareness especially amongst men and strive to make himself a better human being (a lifelong journey in itself) while helping others to be better human beings and change the world one person at a time. Self-reflection and improvement of self starts with taking care of body and mind; the two gifts we are all born with. Nurturing both allows us to share and live wholesome and rewarding lives. Writing, blogging and podcasting allows him to spread meaningful and life changing messages which feed the health of your soul.

Samuel Hatton

Qualifications/Services: Accountability Coach, Behavior Change, Group Facilitation
Location: San Francisco
Website: www.samuelhatton.com

Samuel Hatton helps working-class professionals and freelancers accomplish goals, change habits, and live better. With academic degrees in both entrepreneurship and performance, he's spent thousands of hours facilitating personal growth.

Sarah Ross

Qualifications/Services: Motivational Speaker, Corporate Trainer and Coach
Location: Live in Oxford, UK, Work Internationally
Website: www.YourReasonToBreathe.com

Award winning International speaker, coach and trainer, Sarah Ross, is also the founder of "Your Reason to Breathe", a program that helps people suffering from burnout to rediscover their true purpose and to profit from resilience in both their corporate and personal lives.

As a motivational speaker, Sarah uses the lessons from her own journey back from Burnout and Depression, to being named by the Women's Economic Forum (WEF) as an "Iconic Woman Creating a Better World for All" in 2017.

Her experiences of volunteering at an orphanage for disabled children in Vietnam, provide the foundation for individuals and corporate teams to be empowered to make the changes needed in their lives so that they too can thrive in a sustainable and resilient way. Sarah motivates management and teaches teams to use innovative, creative new approaches to team dynamics to revolutionize how to profit from resilience whilst letting no one burn out in the process.

In addition to working with corporate executives and businesses, Sarah also coaches individuals who need to break the cycle of negative thinking and burnout, to reset and recharge so that they can work towards their own "reason to breathe" in a successful and resilient way. Through coaching and taking part in volunteering projects, she enables her clients to prioritize their purpose, both at home and in the office, so that they too can live the lives that they had never previously thought possible.

Sarah currently lives in Oxford, UK and travels globally to speak to audiences and consult with businesses. Visit her online at www.YourReasonToBreathe.com

Scott Tolchin

Qualifications/Services: Life Coach, Relationship Coach, and Healing Arts Practitioner
Location: Worldwide
Website: SuperfyYourLife.com, Scott@SuperfyYourLife.com
Social Media: https://www.facebook.com/superfyyourlife/

Scott Tolchin is a 21st century mind-body healing arts practitioner and life coach who uses a variety of healing modalities and coaching interventions to help people who are experiencing difficulties related to chronic stress and anxiety, traumatic experiences, stuck emotions, phobias, panic attacks, nightmares, addictions, post-traumatic stress, and chronic inflammation and pain in the body that conventional Western medicine has not been able to alleviate. Scott's mission is to radically transform people's lives in a way that frees them from the pain of their past and empowers them to create new visions for their future and provides them with effective strategies for making that future become a reality while living life fully and vibrantly in the present.

By utilizing the most effective neuroscience-based modalities like Havening Techniques® to rapidly and permanently erase the pain of your past experience, Strategic Intervention Coaching to solve current problems and create new beliefs and behaviors, and hypnosis and NLP to program in your new way of being in the world, you will find that profound change can happen more easily and rapidly than you ever thought possible.

Scott is one of the first 100 Certified Havening Techniques® Practitioners in the world and is a certified Neo-Ericksonian Hypnotist and Master Practitioner of Neuro-Linguistic Programming® (NLP).

Scott is also certified in coaching as a Strategic Intervention Master Level Coach and trained as a Strategic Intervention Advanced Relationship Coach and a Robbins-Madones Core 100 Coach.

Selena Ardelean

Qualifications/Services: Worldwide Facilitator of SHINE
Location: Brussels
Website: www.selenashine.com, www.selenaardelean. com

Selena Ardelean, former teacher and university assistant teacher of English in Romania, emigrated to Belgium in 2003. Mother of 3 awesome boys, wife, restless traveler, Selena is following Joy around the world. She facilitates SHINE Method workshops and sessions where she supports people with understanding the cultural shock, cultural inheritance and familial programming when it comes to limiting beliefs that confine opportunities of personal growth.

Tim Dean

Qualifications/Services: Certified Professional Coach, Executive & Leadership Coach, Millennial Coach
Website: www.thecoachingdean.com
Connect: www.linkedin.com/in/timothyjdean

Tim J. Dean is a recognized global coach, certified trainer and sought-after keynote speaker with a passion for empowering others to realize their full potential. A published author and adjunct professor, Tim coaches individuals, especially Millennials, to integrate their unique business skills with their strong social values so that they can accelerate their career and make a difference in the world.

With extensive business experience in talent management, manufacturing, energy, agriculture and healthcare, Tim brings a unique and powerful mix of strategy, empathy and real-world insights to every coaching engagement.

Tim holds a Master of Science in Industrial Administration from the Tepper School of Business at Carnegie Mellon

University and a Bachelor of Science in Industrial Engineering from Penn State University. Tim's first published work, "Coaching Millennials," is available on Amazon in "Coaching Perspectives V."

Zachary Heidemann

Qualifications/Services: Life/wellness coach, plant walks & herbal medicines, didgeridoo & sound healing
Location: Maryland
Connect: https://www.facebook.com/wildchildmedicine/
Social Media: @treezat

Zachary has seen many paths through his walks of life. Part of his ability to connect in powerfully motivating ways stems from staying humble and leading a relatively ordinary life. Through his life he has dealt with abuse, trauma, addiction, toxic relationships and through it all instead of perpetuating the old people hurting people mentality, he has chosen the path of healing the cycle of people hurting people through loving-kindness, healthy & wholesome disciplines, herbal medicines, didgeridoo, sound healing and more. He has studied many religions including Christianity, Buddhism, Taoism, Islam, Hinduism and more. Through these studies he has come to believe in the universal truths contained within all religions that lead us to skillful relationship with abundance and peaceful prosperity for one and for all. He also practices various combined forms of meditation and yogic and spiritual disciplines extensively and has done this increasingly for over 15 years now. Zachary believes that any system or relationship may be healed through a holistic approach where we can skillfully relate to ourselves to balance our bodies through healthy organic foods and herbal medicines to support conditions for wholesome disciplines of meditation and moving the body and energies in ways that optimize healing and growth and encourage us to cultivate the greatest potential of our being. Through skillful relationship to ourselves and our environments we can create the greatest world of our dreams as realities according to Zachary.

If you enjoyed the book

visit us at
www.activateyourlifebook.com
for exciting updates
and please leave us a review
on Amazon.